From Normandy

To The Hell Of

Ravensbrück

Life and Escape from a Concentration Camp:

The True Story of 44667

Francis Pitard

PAGE PUBLISHING, INC.
New York, NY

First originally published by Page Publishing, Inc. 2016

ISBN 978-1-68348-728-9 (Paperback)
ISBN 978-1-68348-729-6 (Digital)

Printed in the United States of America

INTRODUCTION

To my family and friends around the world

These were the times and places where humans descended to a level lower than animals and *Ravensbrück* was one of those times and places where dignity became an unimaginable luxury. This memoir is a true story; the details are historically accurate. None of the characters are fictional. I, Francis F. Pitard, was born in 1942 near the infamous Normandy beaches. At the time, my great-aunt (on my father's side), Charlotte Aline Virmoux, called Aline, was forty-seven years old. She and her husband, Louis, were active members of the French Resistance. During my youth, I met her on many occasions and learned about her experiences in the infamous German concentration camp, *Ravensbrück*, which was located approximately sixty miles north of Berlin. It was spring 1962, while I was a student in Paris at the Gay-Lussac Institute that I started to appreciate Aline's story and understand who she was. She lived in a small town, Quincy-sous-Sénart, south of Paris where I often visited her. She loved talking with me and sharing her life story. At twenty, I had already heard many war stories from my family, cousins, and friends; but the intensity of these stories never matched the clarity or had the impact on me as Aline's. I hope I can do justice to her memory by delivering this message of when and where horror became routine and people were systematically denigrated and stripped of their humanity.

One weekend during the early sixties and not knowing what to do with my time in *Paris*, I decided to visit her. It was a direct route by train, only half an hour away. I rang the doorbell, which she answered carrying a loaded shotgun and escorted by her German shepherd. The well-trained dog was silent.

"Fanfan! Oh my God!" she exclaimed.

Fanfan was my nickname that my family gave me to keep it straight as to which Francis they were referring as I shared first names with my father and grandfather. After putting the gun down, she wrapped me in her arms and squeezed until I could barely breathe.

"I can stay with you until tomorrow," I said.

"Perfect! We are going to make a feast and celebrate, you and me. You have grown so much since I saw you with your grandparents about five years ago." My grandmother, Helene, was Aline's older sister.

We talked for hours. She never stopped talking as she prepared dinner and continued talking during dinner and never stopped talking after dinner, that is, until about 11:00 p.m. when she stopped talking and became emotional. Suddenly, she started to cry about her horrific memories of the war, of *Ravensbrück*, and of her missing husband, Petit Louis. What she endured in *Ravensbrück* was the Nazi's slow, systematic, and cruel destruction of the human soul and body. The dog came close to her, placed his head on her lap, looked up, and stared into her eyes as if to assuage her pain and tell her he loved her.

I visited her monthly during the next two years. What I learned from her those days had totally, and forever, changed my perspective of humanity. I was stunned and viscerally affected by her reminiscences of the events leading up to and while at *Ravensbrück*—stories straight from hell. I heard anecdotes that nobody could ever imagine, no matter how tortured and imaginative their mind was. As a post-World War II child, I knew of Nazi atrocities but it was in a remote, abstract way. To sit and talk of such horrors face-to-face with a survivor, in the calm of her home—removed by time and distance—amplified the enormity of Nazi atrocities.

Her accomplishments and bravery were gratefully acknowledged by the highest honors anyone can receive from the French, British, and American governments.

For many years, I wanted to write her story. For many years, my relatives and friends asked me to write her story. But I was not ready. Then I came to a point in my life when I started to write historical fiction novels. The first book, *Heirs of a Lost Race*, and its sequel, *Rapa Nui Settlers*, combined with several famous technical books that I authored, increased my writing skills. The exposure gained from those books helped build my confidence. Finally I was ready to write Aline's story.

My sole objective in writing this book is to give voice to just one of the heretofore unknown millions of stories like Aline's. A friend of mine told me once, "You should write this story that was stolen from us." I write because of a passion for it. Therefore, I hope you will enjoy the story, learn something about human existence and condition, and then look at the beautiful life that we have been given with an entirely new perspective. My thinking about mankind has evolved numerous times. At first, I was angry. Then I became sad. Later, I became disgusted. Over the years, I mellowed and became more serene and a peace advocate. Indeed, there is no option for the human race other than having the peace to prosper and prepare for its future. Religions that do not promote peace offer nothing for our souls. Religions that do not respect women's freedom have nothing to sell. Governments who do not respect the freedoms of its people are cancers in this world. Without peace and mutual respect, mankind will never advance. It is the way it is.

ACKNOWLEDGMENT

I am indebted to many people who have supported my work, inspired me, and encouraged me to pursue, day after day, the extraordinary exploration of the human mind during the difficult years of World War II. I am especially grateful to Deloris, my wife, our good friends, Doug Lange and Janet Seahorn, for their efforts to polish the manuscript.

A FEW RELEVANT PICTURES AND NAMES

USS TEXAS, the closest battleship to us on D-Day

D-Day Battleships

- USS *Texas*
- USS *Arkansas*
- USS *Nevada*

- HMS *Rodney*
- HMS *Warspite*
- HMS *Ramillies*

The P-38 Lightning was a very effective and fast fighter, bomber, and reconnaissance plane, especially for precise small targets, such as cars, trucks, tanks, and trains.

The B-17 Flying Fortress, the terror
of small towns in Normandy

CHAPTER 1

Anecdotes

"Mrs. Charlotte Aline Virmoux, declared a few days ago a 'Chevalier de la Legion d'Honneur' for your support for the Allies as a lieutenant of the Evasion Pernod French Resistance Network, and for your exceptional bravery following your escape from the Nazi Germany concentration camp, it is a great pleasure to meet you. I, General Charles De Gaulle, President of France, thank you in the name of the French people for your services and for your valuable contribution to our freedom. My niece, Genevieve De Gaulle, with whom you shared a cell sends you her warmest regards. Madame, it was a great honor for me to make sure my subordinates would give you this glorious medal in the name of the French Republic and the French people."
—General Charles De Gaulle, President of France

That day in June 1961, during a ceremony to honor the old warriors of WWII, Aline would briefly meet Genevieve De Gaulle again. At that time, Genevieve was forty-one and Aline, sixty-six. They embraced each other for a long time and talked with other friends.

"How different you look!" Aline said. "If I did not know it was you, I would never have recognized you."

"The same goes for you!" Genevieve replied laughing.
This was the last time Aline would see Genevieve.

Before I venture into the remarkable life of my great-
aunt and the dark side of Nazi Germany, it is important
that I digress for a few moments and relate a few incidents that happened to my parents when I was a child.
Some I remember vividly, some I was told about. I have
included these incidents as they illustrate the irony of
war, which abounds. Irony starts when you realize the
enemy you face every day may be just another human
with a similar mission... to kill the other guy, but with
similar goals... to survive the war, go on living, raise a
family, and retire in peace. Let's face it, war is stupid
by any definition. It is always the result of mankind's
incapacity to understand the deep, historical motivations
of their adversary. As a result, we generally make a bit-
ter enemy of him. Incompetent and pompous politicians,
many of whom suffer from advanced conflicts of interest, often bear responsibility for plotting the irreversible
courses that inevitably lead to conflict. For thousands
of years, the mantra of madness has repeated endlessly.
Wars must be fought, wars must be won, retribution must
be taken, wars must be fought, *ad infinitum*. We repeat it
even today... in the twenty-first century! Pathetic! Now
I return to the story.

The story begins during February 1943. For chrono-
logical context, the Germans attacked France on May 10,
1940. France signed an armistice with Germany. I was

born in Normandy, in Condé sur Noireau, on February 5, 1942. It was February 1943, in Condé sur Noireau.

It was during a particularly cold evening following a rare snowfall. It was a rare event because of our proximity to the coast. There was no electricity and my mother was struggling to keep us warm. She had complained to my father that she could not keep me warm enough. Close by, there was a train station with a coal stockpile. Unfortunately, it was heavily guarded by German soldiers. My father decided the only solution was to steal some coal. He left home carrying a big sack. He carefully maneuvered closer to the coal pile and waited patiently until the patrols were farthest apart. He then went to the pile and filled his sack as fast as possible. On his way back, he ran into a German patrol that heretofore rarely took that path. He was forced to show the contents of his sack to the soldiers. Because of strict curfew rules, anyone outside at this hour could have been shot. One of the German soldiers recognized my father because he often patrolled near our home during the day. My father explained he was desperately trying to keep his wife and baby warm.

"Go home!" the German demanded, pointing his machine gun at my father's chest. The other soldier took my father's sack away from him.

"If you do this once more, you are dead!" the soldier told him.

A few days later, while my father was at work in an electric motor factory a few miles from home, the German soldier came to our home.

"Eggs!" he ordered, scaring my mother. "Omelet!"

She understood he wanted a respite from his usual army rations. She went to the neighbors and borrowed a few eggs to make an omelet, which she shared with him. He pulled his wallet from his pocket and showed my mother a picture of his wife with a young child on her lap.

"My family! Not seen them since one year."

He got ready to leave and walked over to our stove and opened the top to verify that it was wood being burned, not coal.

"Your husband! No more coal or big trouble."

Then he went away. My parents never saw him again.

A few days later my parents put on their best clothes and went to a nearby café and restaurant to socialize with a few friends. I was at home being minded by a young woman. My mother looked very classy in her dark blue jacket with golden buttons.

A German officer came to their table and asked my mother, "Is Madam German?"

Surprised, nobody knew what to say, including my mother.

"No, I am French!" she finally replied.

"Excuse me!" The German officer replied and walked away.

Indeed with her jacket, golden buttons, and nice blond hair, she very much looked like a woman German army officer.

A few days later the same officer and two other soldiers were patrolling the street where we lived. They asked people questions and searched their homes. What they were looking for wasn't apparent. When the officer entered our home, he saw my father drawing on a map of Europe he had tacked to the wall.

"What are you doing?" the officer asked.

"I follow news on the radio... I find it interesting." My father was a very calm man.

"Yes, very interesting indeed," the officer said, coming closer to the map. He pointed a finger at Stalingrad in Russia.

"This is not good at all! Very bad for Germans."

He shook my father's hand and left to inspect our neighbors' homes.

This was the kind of daily life they had during the German occupation. It was not too bad... as long as simple rules were followed.

It was 4:00 a.m. on June 6, 1944. Seven miles off the Normandy beaches and Pointe du Hoc, the dark hulking outline of the battleship USS *Texas* slowly emerged from the fog that had covered the sea for several days. It slowly and quietly maneuvered parallel to the coast like a specter from another dimension. Five six-hundred-ton turrets, each armed with two fourteen-inch guns, slowly rotated toward the coast. Up and down the one-hundred-kilometer line, five other massive battleships (the British ships HMS *Rodney*, *Warspite*, and *Ramillies*, with the American ships USS *Arkansas* and the famous *Nevada*, the revamped survivor of Pearl Harbor), twenty-three cruisers, and 105 destroyers maneuvered into position along the line of battle. Farther behind the warships waited the largest armada ever set afloat, it consisted of 1,213 support ships waiting to be deployed following the cataclysmic pounding that was to alter Normandy's beautiful landscape forever.

At 5:50 a.m., *Texas* started the deadly barrage that obliterated the coastal landscape. Salvo after deafening salvo wreaked havoc on the once serene seascape, permanently deafening sailors aboard and soldiers on the ground. Each fourteen-inch shell erased an area the size of a football field. During the initial barrage, *Texas* fired 255 fourteen-inch shells in thirty-four minutes, which is an average of 7.5 shells per minute. For miles around, the earth shook as though in a perpetual earthquake for hours, creating a living hell. Despite being well-entrenched, the Germans were unprepared for the magnitude of the onslaught, the location of the attack, and, especially, because of the day's inclement weather.

At the same time, in an isolated farm about two miles inland and south of Pointe du Hoc, my parents were visiting friends who invited them for a wedding ceremony. I was two and half years old. We had stayed at the farm for several days waiting for the weather to clear before departing on their bikes and child's bike trailer to our little home, and birthplace, in a hamlet half a mile off Condé sur Noireau. They had heard from the radio at the farm that several surrounding towns had been bombed by the Allies. They had no idea that Condé Sur Noireau would be erased from the map on the next day just before they returned home.

At 5:50 a.m. the ground convulsed violently causing everything to fall from the walls. My mother ran outside, screaming in the darkness with me in her arms. I vividly recall that moment though I was so young. My father took his binoculars and climbed the stairs to their barn's top floor. The view was an apocalypse—a clone of Hieronymus Bosch's *The Last Judgment*. The coast glowed red with fire. The Allies' massive naval bombardment painted a hellish nightmare on the canvas that was once one of the most beautiful places in Europe.

"One of the big bunkers at Pointe du Hoc just got pulverized!" my father shouted. "I think this is the big day we have been waiting for. Nobody would have guessed it would be there. We are at the wrong place at the wrong time. Let's pack!"

It is well-known that a lucky fourteen-inch shell from *Texas* obliterated the massive German bunker at the top of Pointe du Hoc. Even today, there are several-ton pieces of the reinforced concrete bunker remaining unmoved from where they fell on that fateful day. That lucky shot saved the lives of many brave allied soldiers who had been ordered to attack the Germans on D-Day by climbing the shore's vertical cliffs. To everyone's surprise, the attack was a success.

Soon after the initial bombardment commenced, a German patrol stopped at the farm. An officer came to my father and talked to him in broken French saying, "You take that woman," then pointing at my mother, "and that child. Go now! Schnell!"

There was nothing to argue about. Obviously, the German army would soon regroup and rally in all the surrounding villages and farms in a defensive position. My mother and father took their bikes, the baby trailer, a few provisions, and left for home peddling on rainy, narrow roads, dangerously crossing convoys. There was no doubt that the German officer saved our lives by forcing us to leave early enough before the area turned into the infamous battlefield where too many young soldiers would die. Indeed, years later, the first time I visited the American Cemetery in Normandy when viewing the white crosses and white Star of David that covered hundreds of acres on the quiet rolling hills, I was stunned, heartbroken, and incapable to say a word. It was one of those occasions when the sanctity of profound silence could not be improved with words.

Some twelve thousand Allied troops died on D-Day, of which an estimated 6,600 Americans. The Germans had an estimated nine thousand casualties. But this was only the tip of a much larger iceberg. The carnage on D-Day and the following battle of Normandy that lasted many months claimed a total of 425,000 people killed, wounded, or missing.

On June 5, 1944, five thousand people lived peacefully in Condé sur Noireau. On June 6, they knew about D-Day and rightly worried about it. On June 7, in the morning, their lives were turned upside down. It was a dark day the townspeople would never or could never forget. My parents were still on their way back, on their bikes, having no idea what they would find soon. My parents were living in a small hamlet named *Bouilly* about half a mile east of Condé sur Noireau at the top of a hill where we had moved a few months earlier at a small house owned by some friends, "les Masserons." The couple had a ten-year-old daughter with whom I liked to play. My parents and I returned that evening after a long, exhausting trip and bad weather. But a few hours earlier in Condé sur Noireau the air sirens sounded twice. It was only two Lockheed P-38 Lightning fighter aircraft that passed low and fast—presumably on a reconnaissance mission. Moments later, the third alert came. Many people stayed complacently in their homes, assuming it was another recon flyover… a lethal assumption for many.

As the sirens went off, the distinctive rumbles of a squadron of high altitude Boeing B-17 Flying Fortresses bombers were overhead. Within minutes, the entire town was leveled. Many civilians died that day in our little town, becoming part of warfare's ubiquitous "collateral damage." Even today, the exact number remains unknown. The only structure spared was our church, which remained standing (somewhat). The Allies intended to target German troops and tanks heading to the battlefield as well as taking out the railroad and a key bridge over the river. The place near the river where I was born was no more. My parents found it impossible to bike directly through town due to rubble that blocked the roads, streets, and many trails. They were forced to circumambulate the town via numerous gardens and pastures full of very upset and unfriendly cows. Once they reached home, in Bouilly, they found Mrs. Masseron and her daughter crying and shaking in fright.

They had witnessed the carnage from their vantage point. They saw everything. They heard screaming from everywhere. The stench of blood and gore drifted toward them, permeating the countryside as it moved. Many of their relatives and neighbors, who were still alive under the rubble, moaned and begged God for a quick death.

Others wandered around in shock—deafened, blinded, wounded, mutilated, bleeding, and confused. Even the dogs, cats, and rats were in shock, wandering aimlessly and leaving town in droves. The entire area was covered with a cloud of dust laced with the acrid odor of burning chemicals. It was carnage beyond human imagination. Sadly, many cities, towns, villages, and hamlets throughout Normandy would suffer the same fate. Nearly one million homes in Vire, Caen, Falaise, Le Havre, Villers-Bocage, Saint-Lo, Lisieux, Flers, Mayenne, Domfront, Argentan, and other places would simply cease to be.

We loved our Allied friends! How could they know the extent of their collateral damage? What could they have done other than high altitude carpet bombing? Sadly, massive bombings of everything in enemy territory was an accepted and widely used tactic of both sides. But it seemed ironic that our friends, the Allies, would kill so many of us to kill so many of the Germans. Intellectually, we understood what would be required to pave the road that would ultimately end in Berlin.

The next day, my parents and I left Normandy traveling south to Segré where my grandparents lived. This proved to be a wise decision as the battle of Normandy had just started. It would have been suicidal to stay in the area. As they passed near our town again, not far from where we used to live, my father took a few pictures (see pictures at the end of this chapter). A few weeks earlier, before departing to Bouilly, my parents left our cat, Sapho, with our neighbors who were killed during the bombing. Imagine our joy when Sapho greeted us near one of the few undamaged structures, a bridge.

Ironically, that bridge was the prime target of the bombing. She was bruised, shaking, and begging for a few moments of love and care. Sapho lived a happy life with us for seven more years. It is amazing how little treasures go a long way during dark days like this. Millions of people left the region, having lost everything and with absolutely no hope of rebuilding anytime soon. They were happy to be alive. Most trekked south… going to some nameless destination. Any place was acceptable as long as it was "any place but here." The panic and desperation that engulfed those trying to escape from hell, fueled by mind-numbing rumors, came to be known as "La Debacle." Fortunately my father had a plan and a destination.

It took my parents four days to bicycle the 170 kilometers to my grandparents' home in Segré. Sapho and I bounced along behind my father's bike in our little trailer. Sapho enjoyed my petting her, deigning from time to time to reward me with grateful purrs.

Hoping that we could escape the destruction, we were dismayed to find the town of Flers half-destroyed. My parents interrupted the journey to look for my mother's older sister, who lived near the railroad station. Everything in the area had been leveled. We were unable to find her. Continuing, they passed through Domfront a few hours later—it too had been bombed. Fearing the worst, they went to the small village of Saint Fraimbault where my mother's mother lived with her youngest daughter. Thank God they were okay. We spent the night with them and continued our trip the following morning to the city of Mayenne, named after the large river that split the city. Several bridges that crossed the Mayenne River had been destroyed as were many homes on both sides. It took my parents all day to find a way to cross the river. Eventually they were able to locate and cross in a small boat. They continued south through Laval, the largest city and capital of Mayenne department, then arrived at the small village of Forcé where they met the mayor and stayed overnight. The mayor told them he had a job for them after everything calmed down. They continued their journey all day when, about twenty kilometers from our destination of Segré, my mother could not take it anymore and dozed off while peddling and veered off the road and rolled into a ditch.

"Let me sleep here for the night," she said to my father.

Fortunately it was not raining!

The main street

A factory

The church and a bridge that was
supposed to be destroyed

Sapho before the bombing

The author before the bombing

An old, historic part of the church

Very near to where the author was born

Another factory

Our street

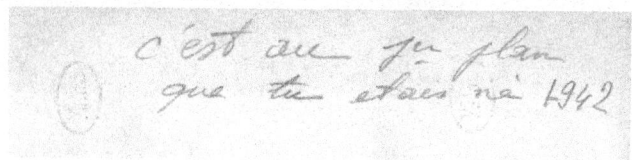

Our house leveled to the ground

Our neighbors' house leveled to the ground

Our friends, les Masserons

Our friends, les Masserons

How is it conceivable that they could smile?
Today, we take a lot of things for granted!

Searching for anything of value

Survivors trying to get organized
It took eight years for the town to
return to normal. Almost!

It was a sunny Saturday in Segre, Maine et Loire on August 1944 (shortly before it was liberated) when the air raid sirens sounded. You would think that by that time we were well-trained. My grandfather, an agent of the French Passive Defense, was responsible for alerting and guiding the town's four thousand residents to take proper precautions and shelter when air raids were imminent. He was assigned to this role because of his authoritarian, strong voice. The local priest had been so impressed by it that he was recruited to sing *Cantique de Noël* (O Holy Night) each Christmas Eve. That afternoon, he assumed that an air raid might shortly take place as a German train carrying V-1 flying bombs (the infamous buzz-bomb) and V-2 rockets moved through the rail yard, stopped, and reloaded coal. Booming his message with great gusto, he ran through the streets of Segré, where he was born.

It was instant hysteria and total chaos. Mothers with babies, teens, old people, the ill, and healthy, even old veterans from World War I, on crutches and in wheel-chairs, charged into the countryside on an old, poor-ly-maintained, half dirt road.

My father, who had been on a fishing trip earlier in the morning, bicycled toward town from the oppo-site direction. Seeing the approaching cloud of dust, he stopped to look at the stampeding crowd.

"What happened? Where are you all going?" he shouted.

An old veteran, sweating mightily in his wheelchair, answered, "There are big bombs on the train! The planes are coming! Everything is going to blow up."

My father, who was well-acquainted with the aerial bombing in Normandy, looked at them in disbelief.

"You do know," he reasoned, "the train station is three kilometers from town. I think you are safe even if the bombs on the train explode."

Panicked, the townsfolk shot past him on their way to a nearby village, Saint Aubain. And here came my mother, with me in her arms. My father tried to reason with her but she was on a life-and-death mission and in no mood to listen to my father.

Biking "upstream" through the throng, my father rode to the upper part of Segré to check on my grandparents.

"I feel like a salmon fighting my way upstream!" he joked to himself.

He found my grandfather and grandmother enjoying a copious lunch on the porch, replete with a good wine from Anjou.

My father started laughing, saying, "Don't you think you went a little overboard making all these people panic?"

"What do you mean? I did my job, didn't I?"

They all tossed their heads backward, roaring in laughter.

Interestingly, on that day, the planes never came!

It was the end of June 1946 in Forcé, a small town south of Normandy, where my parents attempted to build a new life after losing everything in Normandy. My mother managed a little grocery store and café and my father ran the post office. Every morning he was exercising with his bike delivering the mail to all surrounding farms. Nearby there was a large castle and estate (Chateau de Poligné), which was owned by the de Waresquiel family. They had many thousands of acres of apple and pear trees.

When the war was over, the family employed two German soldiers still officially POWs and who dared not try to escape as secret services police were watching very closely. Once in a while, the two Germans would come to the grocery store, that my mother managed, to buy cigarettes or food. One of them did not talk much. The other one, Hans, was more fluent in French and could carry on a basic conversation. They spent most of their time working in the estate's apple orchards.

Our family's weekend pastimes included fishing on the river and hunting in pastures around the castle for wild *Agaricus campestris* mushrooms (a close relative of the cultivated button mushroom, but much more flavorful and tasty) and searching for boletus (penny buns or porcini) mushrooms that grow in the woods behind the castle. Collecting mushrooms was Hans' favorite pastime at his home in East Germany. We once ran into him while gathering mushrooms. He spoke to us and guided us to the good spots. I was four and I recall this very well. Actually, it was Hans who instructed me on the importance of knowing the difference between good mushrooms and dangerous ones. One day, I was a few hundred yards from my parents and saw a big patch of good looking mushrooms on a pile of decaying wood. They also smelled very good and I was proud of my discovery. As I reached for the mushrooms, Hans rushed up to me and explained that these mushrooms were deadly

Amanita phalloid (death caps). He pointed out the distinctive color of the gills, shape of the cup at the base of the stem, and the loose dots on the cap. I never forgot that lesson. My parents walked over and joined us. Learning of my narrow escape, they gratefully thanked Hans for his lesson.

"I have a five-year-old son and a three-year-old daughter at home," he said.

From my early days, I have been passionate about collecting and cooking wild mushrooms. Hans was a good man with simple needs and was very honest. Later in this book, I will relate another anecdote involving Hans that I am sure the reader will find inspiring.

These are enough anecdotes about my childhood in and near Normandy. Now we must carry on with the horrors of Nazi Germany's concentration camps and with the life of an exceptional woman.

Decorations Received by Lieutenant Charlotte Aline Virmoux

Chevalier de la Legion d'Honneur

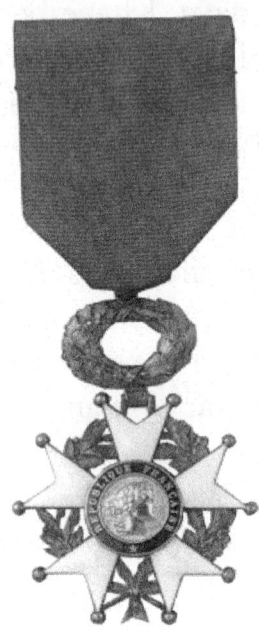

The War Crosses (1939–1945) France

Deportation for Acts of Resistance Medal

Resistance Medal (a medal very dear to General
Charles De Gaulle with "La Croix de Lorraine")

British King George VI War Medal for Courage

The American Medal of Freedom

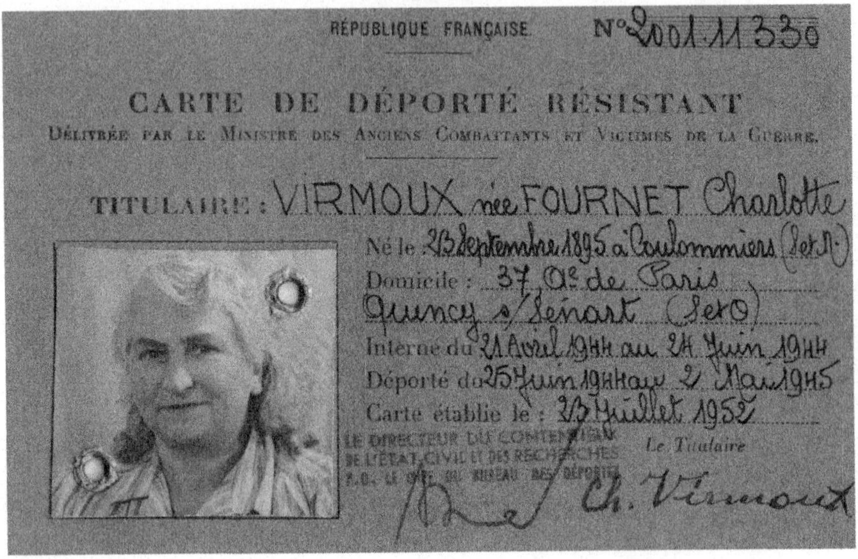
RÉPUBLIQUE FRANÇAISE N° 2001.11330

CARTE DE DÉPORTÉ RÉSISTANT

Délivrée par le Ministre des Anciens Combattants et Victimes de la Guerre.

TITULAIRE : VIRMOUX née FOURNET Charlotte

Né le 23 Septembre 1895 à Coulommiers (Set M.)

Domicile : 37 Av. de Paris

Quincy s/Sénart (Set O)

Interné du 21 Avril 1944 au 24 Juin 1944

Déporté du 25 Juin 1944 au 2 Mai 1945

Carte établie le : 23 Juillet 1952

LE DIRECTEUR DU CONTENTIEUX DE L'ÉTAT CIVIL ET DES RECHERCHES P.O. LE CHEF DU BUREAU DES DÉPORTÉS

Le Titulaire

Ch. Virmoux

Aline in 1952

CHAPTER 2

A Stubborn Young Woman

France, September 23, 1895: Charlotte Aline Elise
Fournet was born in Coulommiers, a small town
northeast of Paris.

The Fournet family was part of a modest, relatively
well-educated branch of French society. Aline's
father worked at a friend's newspaper printing shop.
Her mother was employed as a childcare worker for a
rich Jewish family. Aline had an older sister, Helene
(my grandmother), who was born in 1889 and an older
brother, Emile. Aline hated to be called by her first name,
Charlotte. She was a stocky, healthy girl with a strong
character who resented discipline, which got her into
trouble at school from time-to-time. With her well-de-
veloped sense of right and wrong, she would not tolerate
injustice of any kind.

In May 1906 my grandmother, Helene, who was
an excellent grammarian with a wonderful vocabulary,
dated my grandfather-to-be who was partway into his
two-year training program as a mechanic for the French
railroads. On one Saturday morning during that May, ten-
year-old Aline dressed for her one-hour catechism class

at the local church. She found the class boring, but it was a good occasion to be with her all-girl, good friends. At the time, girls and boys were separated at school and at church.

As the old priest wrote a class assignment on the blackboard, he heard giggling behind his back. At first, he ignored the incident and continued. Then as the giggles intensified every time he wrote on the board, he turned and faced the twenty girls and asked the trouble-makers to identify themselves... stony silence.

"If you don't have the honesty to tell me who is at fault, I will be forced to randomly punish one of you."

Silence.

"Ms. Aline Fournet, please stand up," he ordered.

"I did not do anything!" Aline protested.

"I am not asking if you did anything. I told the class I would randomly choose someone for punishment. Furthermore, I will now punish you even more for your insolence."

Aline could not and would not abide this. She continued to sit on her chair with unabashed disgust flashing in her expressive black eyes.

"Ms. Fournet, stand up with your hands on your head! Today, I will visit your parents and tell them about your unacceptable behavior."

"Is that so?" she replied. "Then I am going to show you something because I will never tolerate injustice."

She walked to the center aisle of the church, her face red with adrenaline. She grabbed her skirt, pulled down her underwear, and urinated on the floor. All the children yelled and screamed in surprise, not believing their eyes.

The priest was taken off guard and, not having an experience like this before, was at a loss on how to handle the situation. Before everyone quieted down, Aline was long gone, running home.

When she arrived at her home crying, she went directly to her father and blubbered what the priest had done to her. She chose to tell her father as he would give a more sympathetic ear than her hot-tempered mother.

"So what?" the father said. "Everyone at your age gets an unfair punishment once in a while. It is not your first time. You never cried like this before."

"Well, perhaps I did something that I should not have done."

"Which is?" her father asked, now becoming more attentive. Her mother and sister listened in on the conversation.

"I got mad, went to the center aisle, and peed on the floor in front of everybody."

There was a long silence in the living room. They all looked at each other. Helene giggled at her mother.

"I don't find this funny," the mother said to Helene.

"You did what?" the father asked angrily.

"I peed on the floor in front of the priest."

The father grabbed Aline by one arm and dragged her back to the church. Aline's feet barely touched the ground. The priest saw them coming, pleased to see her father's anger.

"Young lady, you are going to apologize to Monsieur le Curé now!"

When he let go of her arm, she lost her balance and fell to the ground. She stood up, looked at her father, then at the priest.

"I was punished for something I did not do. You can kill me if you wish, but I will never accept punishment for something I did not do. Yes, I apologize for urinating in front of everyone—but I was angry."

Once more, she ran away crying.

The priest looked at the father.

"You have quite a wild child there, my son. Helene and Emile are angels compared to Aline. How did she turn into this, this feral girl? What are you going to do with her?"

"I don't know. I am truly embarrassed, Father. I will speak to her teacher at school tomorrow."

"I will go to school with you," the priest replied, "because this is not right."

Of course, two days later, the entire town knew about the incident and even a short article was written in the local newspaper about it. Aline's free time with her friends was forfeited for the next three months.

During World War I, Aline's older brother, Emile, was a soldier who fought in the infamous trenches where he saw many of his friends killed. During a battle near Verdun, he was sidelined with a broken leg and nearly killed by Germany's highly toxic, illegal chemical gasses. Like so many other trench soldiers, he never recovered from being gassed and struggled for the rest of his life from the irreparable damage done to his lungs. He died of pneumonia in 1938.

Aline loved her old brother. In his last breath, Aline said, "*Avec la chance, le jour viendra quand j'aurai ma revanche sur ces Boches qui t'ont fait ça* (If I get a chance, one day I will get the bastard Boches who did that to you)."

"Boche" was older French slang for German soldiers during World War I and II.

Shortly after World War I, Aline met a young man in Paris. She was a good-looking waitress at *La Rôtisserie de la reine Pédauque*, a famous restaurant near the Saint Lazarre railroad station. I found it an act of kismet that many years later I would study at the Institut Gay-Lussac, a chemical school, just across the street from the restaurant. The young man, Louis Virmoux, was part of a wedding party. It was love at first sight. Three months later they were married in that little church in Coulommiers, scene of her earlier, but still remembered, indiscretion. Aline was taller and stronger than Louis. He was a relatively short man, five feet five inches tall. She was stoutly-built and five feet seven inches tall. They were unable to have children. They lived a peaceful life near a forest in a little town named Quincy-sous-Sénart, southeast of Paris. They built a house with a large garden, with a gate that led directly to the large and sprawling Sénart forest. One of their passions was hunting for rabbits, pheasants, partridges, and deer. Aline was a very good shot. They shared another passion, collecting wild mushrooms. The Sénart forest abounded with them during summer and fall. Life was good until September 3, 1939. On that day, France, Great Britain, India, Australia, South Africa, and

New Zealand declared war on Germany in response to its invasion of Poland. Like many French during those days, Aline and Louis' only reliable sources of information was from the radio or the weekly newspaper. Louis was a skilled radio technician who worked on radios and built many radio transmitters with my father who had the same trade. They were good friends.

"Now we have to deal with these bastards again," Aline said, fulminating with hatred clearly in her eyes.

"The problem, my dear," Louis replied, "is that we are not nearly as well-equipped to fight the powerful German army this time."

Louis was a quiet, analytical man who rarely became angry. The opposite of Aline who easily lost her temper.

"But, we have many allies," she argued.

"Yes, but they are occupied in other places worrying about the Japanese."

"You are a defeatist!"

Unfortunately, Louis was right. Following fierce battles near Belgium, France officially surrendered to Germany on June 25, 1940. France was no match for Germany's Panzer Tigers II divisions. A few days earlier on June 18, 1940, General Charles De Gaulle gave his famous speech on the BBC radio, calling for the good men and women of France to resist the invader and ignore the Vichy traitors who surrendered.

"France lost a battle, but has not lost the war yet," General De Gaulle said.

"Petit Louis, did you hear this?" asked Aline, who always called her husband "Petit Louis."

"Yes, he is calling for resistance," he replied.

"Petit Louis, we are not going to stay here doing nothing. You have many talents. You have the brain. I want to train to give these bastards total misery. I want to kill the bastards who ruined the life of my brother."

"Calm down, lady. If we are going to do this, it must be done intelligently. We have plenty of time."

For the next three years, Aline and Louis trained to become a subtle part of the Evasion Pernod. This Resistance network was directed and named by Pierre Morel who helped Allied prisoners or wounded Allied soldiers, aviators, and spies to safely return to their homes. The routes taken were carefully guarded secrets and included passage through Germany, Belgium, France, Italy, Switzerland, especially Spain over the Pyrenees, and across the English Channel. They also helped other Resistance networks when needed and were trained to handle light German, French, and Soviet machine guns. They did not carry weapons when out or at home, however they did carry hunting guns. Louis built a radio transmitter in the attic that was used to transmit coded information to the Allies and coordinate the repatriation of Allied troops. As most radio frequencies were monitored by the Germans, there were narrow windows during which he could safely transmit messages to England. It was a very dangerous game. Life and death depended on good timing, but he was very skilled at it.

During September 1941, my parents spent a few days with Aline and Louis. They were married in the village of Saint Fraimbault, Orne department in Normandy where my mother was born. My father's parents attended as well. Many cousins from surrounding farms were present. At the time, my parents were unaware of Aline and Louis' involvement with the French Resistance. My father explained to them what he was doing with my mother as both were working in a factory to build electric motors. Louis was fascinated by the details.

Once, a reconnaissance plane dropped some resistance propaganda pamphlets, my father saw Louis collect a few and study them carefully. My father became concerned.

"Don't get any ideas," my father said. "I disagree with these guys killing Germans and sabotaging things in France. You know the Germans indiscriminately punish us by randomly shooting a few of our men every time one of their soldiers is killed or there is an act of sabotage. Despite his intentions, the killer is at large and the innocents pay the price."

Aline brought a big chicken drumstick to my father and a glass full of *Calvados* for "*Trou Normand*," the *Norman hole*. The "*Trou Normand*" tradition is well-known in Normandy where overindulging feasters may drink a small glass of a hundred and twenty proof *Calvados*, a very hard alcoholic beverage made by fermenting apples to restore their appetites half-way during a ridiculously copious meal. After regaining their appetites, guests would be ready for cheeses and desserts, and more wine and hard cider of course. There were so many apples in *Normandy* that farmers fed them to pigs and dairy cows.

Aline said, "Eat and drink this, Francis, so that the Boche won't get such nice food. Petit Louis is way too smart to get involved in what he is not supposed to."

"This is another thing we should not do. That is keep *Calvados* around. You know the Boche kill to get that stuff to make petrol for their tanks," my father continued.

"If they knew everything I am not supposed to have around here," a farm cousin said, "I would be dead already ten times over. This is one of the nice things about being a farmer—we know the land and we are in a world of our own. Nobody knows about a place like this like we do."

"All these German soldiers are not all bad people," my mother ventured.

"Fernande, please!" Aline snapped, pointing a finger at her. "You are still a child. You know nothing about the bastard Boche. Shut up on this topic and enjoy your wedding."

Everyone became silent.

"Aline is right," my grandfather on my mother side said, "I also got gassed at Verdun, and haven't recovered since."

My mother and her father were very close to one another, so she ceased arguing.

One month later he died of aggravated pneumonia.

But my father could read between the lines. He knew Aline and Louis were involved in the French Resistance and of course they could not tell anyone. It became even clearer two days later when Petit Louis disappeared while riding his bike away from the farm.

"Where did he go?" my father asked.

"He went to visit an electric generator manufacturing plant near *Condé Sur Noireau*," Aline replied.

My father knew better. There was only one plant of that kind in the region, *Vallee de la Vere* where he and my mother worked. My mother wired electric motors with several other skilled ladies. My father did not pursue the topic but wondered what Petit Louis was up to. He found out a few months later.

After wiring, electric rotors and stators were supposed to be immersed in a paraffin bath for several hours to form a good insulation. He also knew that electric motors were regularly sent to Germany for installation in new fighter planes and bombers. One day, he stopped a technician and observed, "You left the rotors in the paraffin bath only fifteen minutes."

The technician did not answer, but went to his direct supervisor. Moments later, my father was summoned.

"What you saw, you must forget," the supervisor said. "We do this only once a week."

"But the motor will burn out after running a few hours."

"This is precisely the point and yes, it can bring down a plane."

"Do you know the price if the Germans find out?"

"Yes, they will kill us all with no trial or qualms."

That evening, my father went home knowing what Petit Louis had been up to. For many weeks he would ponder if they should quit their jobs and join my grandparents who lived about one hundred seventy kilometers to the south. This is what they did after Condé Sur Noireau was destroyed by Allied carpet bombing, especially when my father witnessed several German inspectors auditing the plant as obviously they suspected something. Fortunately, they were unsuccessful to discover any wrong doing. Indeed, it was time to leave.

Louis and Aline Virmoux a few days
before their arrest by the Gestapo

CHAPTER 3

The Price of Radio Communication

The slice of time to transmit and receive messages from England was very short. The Germans fastidiously monitored the airwaves, searching for Resistance transmissions. One day, Louis Virmoux pushed his luck too far. Some said he was betrayed by neighbors who knew what he was doing. We never learned the truth.

It was April 21, 1944. The weather was cool and rainy at Aline's home. The Allied invasion of Normandy would take place only a few weeks later. Aline had skinned and butchered three rabbits that Petit Louis shot in the forest the evening before. While out hunting, Petit Louis met a man and woman at a very old oak tree, a Resistance landmark where they gave him a coded message to be radioed to England. Moments later, Petit Louis bumped into a neighbor who was in the forest looking for wild mushrooms.

After Aline had finished the rabbits, they decided to have breakfast in the kitchen before she cleaned everything up. At the end of breakfast, she grabbed a large apple.

"Petit Louis, do you want to eat half an apple with me?"
"Yes!"

She twisted the apple in half with her bare hands!

Minutes later, Petit Louis went to the mailbox and came back with the weekly newspaper. He sat in the kitchen reading and commenting on the important news to Aline, who was busy washing dishes. Then she started mopping the tile floor.

"Petit Louis, go read the paper in the living room!"

He did not answer and continued reading an article about deer hunting in the Sénart forest.

"Petit Louis, move over!"

There was no answer.

"I am going to fix this," she mumbled to herself.

She grabbed the chair—with Petit Louis still sitting on it—and took the full load to a comfortable spot where she deposited him, still reading the paper. As Petit Louis continued reading, a faint smile formed on his face as though nothing had happened. Aline continued the mopping... she was a very strong woman!

"Men!" she mumbled to herself, scrubbing the floor until it shined like a mirror.

Aline and Louis usually ate a light meal in the kitchen, without alcohol. But they always ate dinner in the living and dining room using their best dishes and silverware. The meal was always accompanied by a classy red wine. Petit Louis told Aline many times that this routine was the way to have a good life together. They would talk for hours, always enjoying their time together—they truly loved one another. Both were far from perfect. However they accepted each other's flaws and idiosyncrasies without question.

On that fateful day, Louis went to the attic after dinner. He made a brief radio transmission that outlined the escape plan for an American pilot whose plane was shot down near Germany. The pilot had parachuted and landed near a thick forest in the Ardennes. The pilot was met by members of the French Resistance who smuggled him through a series of safe houses, protecting and caring for him until they reached the Normandy coast. French fishermen took the pilot halfway across the channel at night and met fishermen from England. Good timing was everything, and this was what the coded message was all about.

"Where were you?" Aline asked in a loud voice.

"In the attic," Louis responded.

"Another one of those brave kids?" Aline asked.

"Yes, it is all set. But I may have stayed a little too long on the radio. I was just at my time limit."

"Don't worry, you are smarter than those bastards," Aline replied.

Twenty minutes later, the doorbell rang. Petit Louis went to the door with their dog. Immediately, two German soldiers pushed him aside and burst into their home. A Gestapo officer handcuffed Louis. Louis' dog protested and was shot by the soldiers. Aline stormed to the rescue like a banshee, but she was no match for the Gestapo goons. They handcuffed Aline and proceeded to ransack the house looking for the radio and any incriminating material. The German soldiers searched the house, found the radio transmitter in the attic, and destroyed it. Louis and Aline were roughly shoved into the back seat of the Gestapo's black Citroen 15-6, which was escorted by two motorcycles. A drive to the gates of hell. A neighbor watched the car's dim lights vanish into the cold night.

Early the next morning, after a sleepless night in her cell, Aline heard the German interrogator yelling at Petit Louis in the next room. Obviously, he was getting no information about the Resistance network from the brave little man. Then the Gestapo did what they did best. At regular intervals, Louis screamed in pain.

"The bastards are torturing him," she murmured to herself. "They know nothing about international laws, or they don't want to know and they don't care. Dear God!"

Farther down the cellblock amidst all the screaming, shouting, and crying, Aline could hear the results of the Gestapo's craft as women and men babbled and screamed proclamations of innocence and disclosures of secrets. Clearly, torture worked and had become a refined art in that place.

She tried to open the door, but it was locked and heavily guarded.

"I want to go to the bathroom!" she yelled. But there was no answer.

"I want to go to the bathroom!" she repeated louder.

She heard a German coming to the door.

"Go in your pants, bitch!"

"Sure! What did I expect?"

Then Louis's screams cut through the cacophony and became more intense and deeper as though he was being suffocated. The sounds coming from Louis were inhuman, grotesque, and frightening—then he went silent for too long.

A soldier opened the door to Aline's cell and grabbed her. With her hands still handcuffed behind her back, the guard strong-armed her into Louis' interrogation room and slammed her into a chair.

"Now, madam, it is your turn," a Nazi officer said.

When she saw Petit Louis, she burst into tears.

"What have you done to him?"

"It would have been wise for him to give the requested information."

"You would kill him anyway."

"Possibly!" Louis's hands and neck were a mass of cigarette burns. His eyes were swollen closed, they were bluish-black and bleeding. Blood dribbled from where Louis once had fingernails. And one of his ears was missing.

He was in a coma but still breathing. She could tell because of the blood bubbling from his nose.

"Now the question is," the German said, "did you know about your husband's activities?"

"Yes, he is a self-employed radio-electrician."

"This is not what I asked," the German replied, back-handing her face.

Strong primal emotions kicked in, she did not flinch one iota.

"Who and where are the collaborators who work with you? I want the list."

The German took his cigarette and pushed it into her arm, she did not flinch.

"I know nothing about what you ask," she replied, looking at him with intense hatred and defiance in her dark eyes.

"I know you are lying, bitch," the German replied, slapping her along the side of her head. She thought her eardrum would explode. Again, she did not flinch. Aline laughed at him.

"So an arrogant bitch on top of everything," he laughed in turn. "Let me put it another way."

He came close to her, grabbed a handful of hair from the back of her head, and yanked her head backward. She could not defend herself with her hands tied behind the chair.

"I want you to officially condemn your husband's resistance activities."

"*Jamais, fils de putain*! (Never, son of a bitch!)"

"I am losing my patience with this woman," he said.

He walked around his desk, then came back.

"I want you to condemn your husband's resistance activities," he said calmly, as he moved his face to within inches of hers.

"Never!" she yelled and spat in his face.

It took him a few seconds to slowly wipe the spittle from his face. Placing the towel on his desk, he called for another Gestapo officer to join them. It was the same man who had come to their home earlier.

"Make sure Ravensbrück takes care of that woman. She is a conspirator. As for this man, we are not finished with him yet."

The Gestapo officer gave her wallet and identification cards back to her.

"Don't lose this or you will be shot on arrival!"

As Aline was led away, she glanced back at her Petit Louis, a gentle soul who believed the simple things in life were the best.

This was the last time she would ever see Petit Louis. The Gestapo tortured him again and again for several days. When they were finished, they made him strip to his underwear and loaded him into the back of an army truck loaded with other prisoners. A few days later they were driven to a rail yard. Along the way, members of the French Resistance followed them, hoping to ambush the truck and free the prisoners. Unfortunately, they weren't able to seize an opportunity to attack. They saw the prisoners being packed like animals into the cattle cars. One of them actually saw Petit Louis—still barely alive. It was a cold, rainy day when the soldiers pushed and piled hundreds of grossly underdressed prisoners into each car. The car's doors were closed and locked. Escape from what was called the *Train of Death* was impossible. Even if they could open the doors, the prisoners' deplorable physical conditions left them unable to fend for themselves and survive for even a half day in the cold. They were heading to an unknown concentration camp where those, who still lived, would be further tortured. By the grace of God, many would perish during the days to follow depriving the Nazi sadists their fodder. The horrors depicted in apocalyptic paintings from the Middle Ages presaged the cattle cars and camps.

The lack of water, food, sanitation, and any rudimentary medical care, combined with the pressure from stacked and standing bodies, the pervasive stench of urine and human excrement, oozing and festering wounds, colds, pneumonia, and the deadly fumes from the locomotive gave little chance for survival. Upon arriving at Dachau, the Nazis dumped the dead into mass graves or crematoriums and resumed torturing those who survived. Like so many during those days, Petit Louis ceased to exist. Although he most likely died in the cattle car, his one-line obituary was written in the official records of Dachau as having died in the camp.

CHAPTER 4

The Cattle Train—
Deuxieme Partie

Before the war, most people liked crossing France and Germany by train, enjoying the peaceful and beautiful countryside. During the war, trains taking prisoners to concentration camps became the antithesis of earlier idyllic trips and a harbinger of something far worse. Along the way, many would die due to the Nazi's calculated, deliberate, and cruel way of minimizing the number of unhealthy prisoners they had to keep in the camps. The inhumane shipment of people in trains, the genocidal camps, and brutal slave labor forces combined with Germany's final solution—the extermination of Jews—were designed to create the future of home of the Aryan super race.

After leaving the interrogation center and Louis, Aline and many other women prisoners were gathered at the railroad station for their fateful trip to Germany on June 19, 1944. Some of these women were arrested because of similar activities with the French Resistance. Like the victims of Middle Ages witch hunts, some of the prisoners were arrested because someone who did not like them contrived a charge and denounced them to the Gestapo. Others were caught violating the mandatory evening curfew, selling food or alcohol on the Black Market, being arrogant to a German soldier, or being at the wrong place at the wrong time. Actually, any trivial reason was a good one. Two weeks after D-Day, the Germans became far more paranoid and aggressive as they already saw defeat on the horizon. During that time, the Nazis crammed Aline and sixty other women prisoners into a specially labeled black railroad cattle car located in the middle of a long train, packed into the car like animals being taken to a slaughterhouse.

A cruel blow from the butt of a machine gun and the classic "schnell, schnell!" was the rule. They ranged in age from eighteen to sixty-five. All of their outerwear had been confiscated. They were allowed to wear only very light clothes, wholly inadequate for the cold nights in the drafty cattle car. They could not take any luggage, purses, or any documents besides an identification card. They were not allowed to wear socks and had to endure the roughness of their shoes. The Nazis even took their shoelaces. It was cold and raining, making it even more miserable. Parisians, waiting for other trains, looked at them with pity but there was nothing they could do. The car was full yet they continued pushing more women in. The doors were closed. Aline was on one side of the car, her back against the wooden wall, which was covered with steel mesh screening to thwart any escape attempts. It was very dark in the car; there were no windows or openings. The only fresh air came through small vents in the roof that were also protected by wire mesh. Squeezed between the wall and other women, she could not even move her arms.

"I was supposed to go on a honeymoon tomorrow," one woman joked.

Some laughed. Many were too traumatized to listen.

"I need to go to the bathroom," one woman said.

"Where are the bathrooms?" Aline asked. "Someone please let her know where the toilets are."

This time, everyone within earshot laughed. Despite the attempt at gallows humor, they somberly recognized that the problem would not go away and that their "inconvenience" was part of a sadistic plan. They slowly realized the Nazi's intent was to dehumanize them initially by degrading their dignity, later it would become worse. Within a few hours they would all be in the same situation as that woman.

Realizing that sooner or later everyone would need to relieve themselves, Aline suggested, "Can we try moving in a different way so we have space for a few of us to sit down at times, taking turns, and also relieve yourself at only one place?"

Everyone shifted position to a different angle and formed one row along the wall. The next row then jockeyed for a position between the women of the first row, saving space. They successfully made enough room where about ten women could sit at a time, reserving one corner of the car for their imaginary toilet where they could make compost for the Germans.

"I hope none of you is a lesbian," joked one woman.

"I am!" one woman replied. "But I lost my appetite."

"My name is Louisette," said the young woman standing next to Aline. She was twenty-two, blonde, and good looking. For the record, Louisette Van der Heyden born on September 9, 1922, at St-Eloy-les-Mines (44635) or, at least, it is a guess since there was only one Louisette officially listed as having been on that train.

"I am Aline, from the Evasion Pernod Resistance Network. Nice to meet you, kid!"

The woman smiled at Aline's statement and the reassuring warmth of her introduction. I personally recall Aline used the English word "kid" when she would talk to a person much younger than her. I have no idea when and where she developed such a habit.

"How long do you think we are going to stay sealed in this cattle car?

"I don't know," Aline replied. "It depends where we go in Germany."

"Ravensbrück," Louisette replied.

"Where is Ravensbrück?" Aline asked, vaguely remembering the German interrogator's mention of that name to the Gestapo officer.

"It is on the other side of Germany, north of Berlin."

"Then, it may take us two or three days at best," Aline said.

Those women standing near Aline heard her conjecture, soon it was echoing through the car—the sixty voices roaring their protestation were drowned by the noise of steel wheels on the rails. Apart from not being mentally prepared for their journey, none were prepared for the physical abuse, the cold humid weather, nausea from the heavy fumes from the train, the endless click-clacks on rail joints, and abrupt shifting of the car as it sped through the countryside. The metal-on-metal screeching, whistle blowing, and women's plaintive lamentation were mind-numbing assaults on their ears and brains. This in itself was enough to make anyone sick. Nerves were on edge, tensions rose, and gratuitous insults began to demonstrate that the prisoners' mental health was deteriorating fast. The Gestapo's mind-manipulators well knew how this environment could degrade prisoners' dignity, driving them to a point where even the strongest would no longer be able to logically analyze and react to their situation.

To those who were enjoying normal lives in the countryside they were zipping through, one day went by, to those in the cattle car, it was a lifetime. The dark dreariness of the days and the lack of windows made it difficult to tell whether it was day or night. The frequency of the train's click-clacks slowed and the car's corresponding banking indicated curves in their route. Adding to the prisoners' angst, low-flying planes—well-known for attacking trains in Germany or anywhere else if they were suspected of carrying ammunition or supplies to the German army—added another level of psychological stress. The train went through a tunnel. Instantly the car was filled with deadly fumes. Everybody coughed and desperately pressed clothes or rags over their noses and mouths to filter the air they breathed. Several women lost consciousness. Still standing, Louisette put her head under Aline's arms to escape the fumes.

"You would not have done that when I was gardening in summer!" Aline thought aloud.

Aline covered her nose with Louisette's long hair. They could tell that the train was slowing by the decrease in rail noise. They apparently had exited the tunnel and were coming to a stop. Surely, they thought, someone would open the door and let fresh air enter or bring them badly needed water and food. But, nothing happened. Suddenly they felt the impact of a connecting locomotive, which seemed to push them backward. Minutes later, the train rolled backward. Everyone was concerned about going through the tunnel again, but this time, there was no tunnel. The train stopped and lurched forward again. They guessed their car had been transferred. They could not tell if it was to another train or to another locomotive; it was hard to guess which.

Another day went by. So far, two elderly women died during the trip. It was too much for them. They were unable to cope with the rigors and deprivations to which they were subjected. Many more prisoners were now coughing their lungs out, others suffered from badly infected wounds caused by Gestapo beatings. The stench of human urine, sweat, and excrement mixed with the smell of blood, infection, and primal fear was nightmarish. Some of the women were keeping a strong, proud face. But the majority's humanity was deteriorating, they were giving up hope. They screamed, yelled, argued over nothing, and would readily surrender their last shred of dignity for anything that would make them feel better, even if it were for only a minute.

The train came to another stop. This one was much longer. Outside, German soldiers could be heard. They even heard machine guns. Then there was a long silence.

The train moved backward again for a few minutes, came to a stop, then they felt a tremor as they connected to another train. They were being transferred again. The train went backward again. It seemed they were going to retrace their route. This was probably an illusion as the track seemed to curve, head north, and then east again. But this was all guesswork as they had no reference points. The train went through more tunnels. Fortunately they were short on this segment of the journey. By now, most of the women suffered from severe dehydration. Even Aline's fortitude was flagging, she felt sick to her stomach, had a fever, and she battled a furious sinus headache. Louisette slept deeply on Aline's chest. She had found the perfect pillow.

"Sleep, kid," Aline murmured to Louisette. "We will get out of this shit!"

"She is dead!" one women screamed.

"Shut up!" another one replied.

Louisette woke up.

"My throat hurts!" she said. "Where are we?"

"Going to a vacation on the North Sea shore," Aline joked.

"It is not funny!"

"I know, kid. I am well aware we are going to hell. Otherwise they would have given us water and food."

Aline's head pounded. She was no longer in a mood to talk or to listen. Their lengthy water deprivation and train fumes were taking a toll. She tried to save energy and keep her spirits higher by imagining the trip would end soon. But the train kept going and going. Another day went by then the train rolled to a stop. They heard doors being opened on the other cars. They heard German soldiers shouting, hurrying the women, with their usual shouts, "*Schnell! Schnell!*" Screams and lamentations filled the air. Obviously, more cattle cars filled with women had been added to the train along the way.

Louisette Van Der Heyden was fluent in German and said, "They asked the women to line up in rows," she said.

Then the doors to their car were opened suddenly. Without warning, the Germans yanked the women from the cars with unexpected brutality. The soldiers used German Shepherds to harass and threaten the prisoners as they debarked, staggering on weak legs down wooden ramps to a landing. One dog growled threateningly at Aline. Knowing dogs well, she immediately turned her head and looked away. As she stepped from the ramp to the landing, she twisted her ankle. There were bodies everywhere. Bodies littered the ground, yet more were being pulled from the cars and left for the disposal crews. One woman broke from her row and ran only to be killed by a shot to her head. Louisette glanced at Aline. Words could not describe the terror.

"Let's try to stay together," Louisette said. "I feel better with you nearby."

"My pleasure, kid!"

A dog growled at them again. Apparently, talking was *verboten*. It was the middle of the night before the prisoners were finally formed up. They were marched on a muddy road for a long time and passed through a small deserted village. As they walked through the gloom, they looked up and saw the camp's intimidating ten-foot walls, barbed wire fences, and heavily manned and guarded towers. Aline noticed that many of the barracks had a few small windows, which were covered with screens and bars. The camp was sprawling. Several large buildings were at the camp's center. She saw another structure, with chimneys that made it look like a smelter; it emitted a steady stream leaden with noxious smoke, the stench of which was terrible… like burned meat.

They eventually arrived at one of the large buildings and were pushed into a huge, empty room. A German female soldier came to them and looked at them one-by-one.

"Did you have a good trip, bitches?" she asked in bad French.

One prisoner looked at the guard and was roughly slapped for the infraction.

The guard announced, "There are fundamental rules to follow in this wonderful resort. There are humans and animals. We are humans, you are not. You are lower than the animals. You are going to be toys for SS's entertainment. Forget hope, especially those of you from the French Resistance. There is no hope when you pass through the gates of this hell. This is where you are, in hell! You will lose your name. You will lose your personality. You will lose your dignity. You will be tortured until you give names and places of interest to us. You will lose your body. You will lose your mind. Your soul will be destroyed, little by little. A time will come when you will beg for death."

Louisette took Aline's hand then dropped it, afraid of the consequences. This was not good!

CHAPTER 5

Introductions

The cloying smell of burned meat permeated the air, tainting every breath. The camp was clean, but intuitively, they knew something was very wrong about this place. During their march between the train and the reception room, where the women now waited, they already witnessed many SS depravities and disregard for human life. Clearly, their new masters enjoyed killing and inflicting suffering. Worse than having been trained for this, some enjoyed the role of sadistic bully.

Standing in the reception room, the prisoners were told to remove their clothes and shoes. One SS guard and several subalterns went to each of them and collected their wedding rings, earrings, necklaces, bracelets, and watches. All their clothes and belongings were tossed in a large bin. Then, one by one, they went to a room where three women guards waited for them.

Aline had not been able not remove her wedding ring for years as her fingers had become fatter. The SS woman took up a pair of pliers and growled in a terrible French, "You better remove it bitch or your finger is gone!"

Aline spat on her finger several times and finally tugged the ring off.

Thinking in silence, "Oh, Petit Louis, forgive me."

Aline resisted when two guards grabbed her. She was quickly brought under control by the twenty-five lashes energetically applied to her bare back. Never in her life had she felt so much pain.

"Open your mouth, bitch!" commanded one SS guard.

When she didn't immediately respond, one of the German Shepherds bit into her ankle. She yielded and opened her mouth. The third guard, probably a nurse, put a device in her mouth to jack it open, wider and wider, until she felt her temporal-mandibular joint pull apart. The pain was excruciating. Aline had two gold crowns. The guards inserted gore-covered pliers around the device and twisted off the two crowns. She was then shoved into the next room. Aline's mouth was full of blood and her back was shredded.

"Next!" yelled a guard as the prisoners were pushed into an adjacent room where two women and four men waited for them. And, one by one, the four men laid each prisoner on a table, face up, holding the prisoner's arms and legs so she could not move. Then the two women shaved all the hair from the prisoner's body, including pubic hair, with no reluctance whatsoever. Any woman who complained about their indignity would be lashed until bloody.

After the shaving, they were checked for lice. Any woman suspected of having lice or any other skin diseases was moved to a separate group. These women would never be seen again. The remaining women were then showered and bleached. After which they were given prison uniforms that consisted of a loose robe with gray and white stripes that had obviously been used many times before. They were given an apron that was to be worn when performing heavy labor, a pair of very old wool socks, and a pair of shabby sandals. Then in single file, one by one, they stood in front of a desk where a clerk sat with a register. The clerk mechanically entered each prisoner's name in the register, confiscated their identity cards that had been taken from their clothes, and assigned a five-digit identity number to each woman. Aline became 44667, Louisette became 44635. They were also given a red badge with the letter *F* (which stood for French political), which they had to sew on their uniforms. For some reason, the French political prisoners were separated from Jews and prisoners from other countries. The guards also separated criminals, prisoners of war, and women belonging to various resistance groups from each other.

The SS woman who had brutally beaten Aline spoke, "You have been given a number. This is your new name— what are you doing?" she barked, viciously pointing her whip at Louisette's chest.

"I am translating what you said in French for them."

"You were not asked to do this."

"I am sorry. I thought they needed to understand what you said."

"Then continue to do so. Be careful about what you say, I know French a little. At times, I will need your talents."

Louisette, who had family in Holland, was fluent in German. She was surprised at the SS woman's reaction as she anticipated capital punishment.

"Listen to the rules because I will not repeat them twice. The French Resistance bitches will be in barrack thirty-one. There are already many French bitches there. In the morning, you will be assigned tasks to do. Inside the barrack, you can talk to each other but never outside or at work. When answering your guards, you must refer to your number never your name. If you look at the guards at any time, twenty-five lashes. If you look at the dogs at any time, they are trained to bite you. If you rest at work, fifty lashes. You cannot, under any circumstances, relieve your bladder or bowels at work. Go in your clothes if necessary. If you are doing any task other than the one you were assigned, you will be lashed until you are in a coma. However if you accuse any other prisoner of an infraction, you will be rewarded with special privileges. You will be given one bowl of water a day. You can drink or wash with it as you wish. You will be given one bowl of soup every day. At work, you will be given more water. Now, get out of my way."

They were moved to another room where they were provided with water and soup. The soup was very clear and had one chunk of turnip floating in it. A few months earlier, some might have called it a *consommé*.

A few women were removed after being quarantined for three days—they were never seen again. Finally Aline's group was taken to barrack thirty-one. The guards unlocked the door and pushed them forward, locking the door behind them. It was dark. They could barely see the few women who stood and stared at them. Surveying the darkness, Aline saw some of the residents were sleeping on crude, suspended wooden bunks, two women per bunk.

"There are places for you at the other end," one of the women said.

Aline and Louisette found an empty bunk.

"It smells like shit!" Aline said.

Without any discussion, they lay on the primitive bed and immediately went to sleep, a long-awaited luxury.

At dawn, the women were awakened by sirens and told to line up outside for roll call. Each woman was given another bowl of soup; then, depending on how they looked, they were assigned their respective tasks. Aline and Louisette were given shovels and taken some distance away and told to dig a trench. It appeared to be for the foundation of a new barrack. There was plenty of space for new barracks.

Most women in their crew had been at the camp for a long time. They were skin and bones, looking much older than they really were. Most had lost their teeth due to malnutrition. Nearly all showed physical exhaustion and had infected wounds, their skin perpetually covered with a thin layer of dirt. Many had deep, haunting sadness in their eyes. They all cowered in the presence of the guards and dogs.

One woman collapsed on the work detail, totally exhausted. Lash after brutal lash goaded her to stand and avoid any further whippings. Then the lady looked to the heavens, then down at the ground. Trancelike, she went through the motions hoping to escape a further beating.

But in her weakened condition, it was just too much for her to take. Once again she collapsed to her knees then to the ground, moaning from unbearable pain. Without hesitation, the guard shot her in the back of her head.

"*Les salauds!*" Aline murmured to herself, "Blooming bastards!"

The day dragged on with no further incidents. Returning to their barrack, they sipped some of their water ration and washed with the rest of it. The guards locked the doors again. That second evening, Aline and Louisette went around the barrack introducing themselves and meeting other women. Louisette met an earlier acquaintance, a very attractive young woman who had been at the camp for only a few weeks.

"Aline," she said, "I want you to meet a good friend of mine."

"Genevieve," the woman said.

"Genevieve de Gaulle," Louisette added, "niece of General Charles de Gaulle."

Aline looked the woman straight in the eyes with great surprise.

"It is an honor to meet you, kid!"

Both young women smiled.

"Don't worry," Louisette added, "these are Aline's ways."

"How did you end up in that mess so young?" Aline asked.

"I joined the Resistance when I was nineteen in 1939," Genevieve replied, "and how about you?"

"My husband and I are part of the Evasion Pernod Resistance Network's radio communication with

England. One night they caught us. I don't know where my husband is. The only thing I know is they tortured him severely before my eyes. Afterward, I was sent to the cattle car. This is where I met Louisette."

"You must meet a few other women," Genevieve said.

They walked along the rows of suspended beds to a middle aged woman.

"This is Lady X," Genevieve said. "She is our spy. She has access to the SS because she is their hairdresser. She knows German but they don't know that. She listens to many conversations then tells us what is going on."

That night, Lady X described hideous atrocities being committed by German doctors on a group of Polish girls. They were selected because they were healthy, young, and between the ages of ten and sixteen. Once under the control of the doctors, they were subjected to heinous operations—all without anesthesia. The Nazis made deep cuts into some of the girls' limbs and sewed-in germ-ridden rags to study how their immune systems would respond. Others were subjected to horrific mutilations of their arms and legs. For example, a leg might be amputated from one girl and attached to another whose corresponding leg had been amputated earlier, and vice versa. Obviously, many would not survive the operation or, if they did, they lived a few days in horrible agony before they died. The few who did survive were mutilated for life and subjected to additional experimentation—until their ravaged bodies finally gave up. It was not uncommon to see one of these girls, victims of Nazi's medical experiments, crossing the camp, hopping as best they could with their improvised crunches. They were nicknamed the *little bunnies*.

Tears started to form in Aline's eyes as she said in a quavering voice, "I cannot take these atrocities. We had another woman shot in the head today. These bastards have zero compassion."

"As far as they are concerned," Genevieve said, "we are terrorists because France signed a peace pact with them, and you know what my uncle thinks of this."

"I disagree," Aline argued. "The *little bunnies* are no terrorists, yet the Nazis still have zero compassion for them. These bastards are cruel to the bone. Human suffering does not concern them. I see they truly enjoy watching women die, or watching women beg for death."

"I agree," Genevieve sadly added.

Aline, being physically and mentally tough, prepared her mind each morning before roll call for the day's ordeals. Every day, a new barbarity would challenge her sense of injustice. Every day, she knew she would die a terrible death if she slipped up and succumbed to her primal instinct to right wrongs.

A few days later, Aline and the others witnessed a horrifying example of Nazi abominations, one they would never forget. Women were not allowed to have children at Ravensbrück; however, some of the prisoners arrived already pregnant. Fetuses of women who were several months pregnant were aborted by the Nazi's in the most savage manner. Fetuses and the mothers' internal organs were brutally pulled from the mother's womb by bare hands. The fetuses were dumped in garbage cans and sent alive to the crematorium. Some were even buried alive or bayonetted, all in front of the mother. The majority of victims died from internal bleeding and infection. The camp guards had no compassion. They seemed to derive a sadistic pleasure from causing or watching suffering at its malevolent worse.

"The devil looks like an innocent little boy, compared to these guys," Aline once said.

As the prisoners collected dead wood from a nearby forest under heavy SS supervision, one young woman obviously six or seven months pregnant fell to the ground. The guard viciously lashed her until she stood. Upon standing, her eyes rolled back in her head and she collapsed. One of the guards ordered her to crawl. As she crawled, she complained of a pain in her womb. The SS guard told her he would relieve the pain and kicked her with his boots and rolled her onto her side with his feet. He pulled his pistol, aimed it at the side of her abdomen, and pulled the trigger. The bullet went all the way through and came out on the other side of the poor woman. Because of the bullet's trajectory, it was clear the unborn baby had been killed. The woman slumped, moaning incomprehensibly, probably begging for a quick death. She was taken to the crematorium in a wheelbarrow and thrown in.

Later in the evening, Aline, Louisette, Genevieve, and others discussed what they had witnessed. They had all seen a lot of cruelty since their arrival, but what they witnessed that day in the forest was among the worst.

"We really should change the conversation," Genevieve suggested. "Compared to many of you, I am a weak woman. However, if I concentrate on nice memories it helps me cope with our unbearable fate."

Aline was chewing on an old piece of cloth then sipped her leftover water.

"You have a point, kid!" she replied. "But I cannot help thinking that one day, when the opportunity is right, I am going to kill one of them."

"Don't think that way," Louisette protested. "They would most certainly kill you."

"Louisette is right," Genevieve said. "You must stay alive. This is the only way we will win this battle."

"You know what, ladies? You talk like my husband, Petit Louis."

"Then when you are in that stage of anger, Aline," Genevieve suggested, "think about what Petit Louis would tell you to do."

Aline stretched out on her wooden bunk bed and stared at the other bed above her.

"I have a problem with my temper," she admitted. "It's going to kill me."

"I won't let that happen to you," Louisette said, holding her hand. "I will help you."

The woman in the bed next to them moaned in pain. Earlier that day she received fifty lashes. She could not lie on her back and sprawled, naked, on her stomach. The lashes she received that day cut deeply into healing wounds from earlier lashings. She slowly turned her head and faced Aline.

"Every time they can find an excuse to destroy you," she said, wincing, "they win. Remember, this is what they want."

Aline got up, went to the bed, and inspected her wounds. She went to Genevieve and another lady, Germaine.

"What can we do to clean that mess on her back?"

They went to Lady X and asked if she could think of something.

"Tomorrow I will try to bring some cotton and cologne from the shop. In the meantime, take this left-over water and this clean piece of cloth. It is all I have."

They tried to clean the deep oozing wounds as best they could to keep the infection from spreading. But her blood had already been in contact with her filthy garment for too long. It was difficult to help the poor woman escape the devastating consequences of her wounds without proper medical care. Many of the prisoners were carriers of Staphylococcus looking for victims.

"I heard spiderwebs can protect an open wound," Lady X suggested.

"And where on earth do you want me to find spiderwebs?" Aline replied.

"I have not been with my man for a year," one woman said. "I have a fairly good idea where you can find plenty of them."

Aline glanced at Germaine who, in turn, glanced at Genevieve, and they all threw their heads backward and laughed heartily. Even the poor lady in pain could not resist a gentle laugh as well.

"By the way," Aline asked, "what did you do to deserve fifty lashes?"

"I was trying to pick a little violet for Jacqueline's birthday. She's one of my friends at the end of the room."

Aline looked at Genevieve and Germaine.

"I am telling you I am going to kill one of them!"

"By the way, my name is Germaine Tillion. I have been here since 1942 and I know many tricks you will need to know to survive. I am an anthropologist."

"Well, I think you are a well-educated kid," Aline replied, "How old are you?"

"I am thirty-seven."

"My God, I thought you were ninety!" Aline blurted.

"In a few months we may look like twins," Germaine replied with a wry smile. "And by the way, I think you need to go on a diet!"

The other ladies laughed, including Aline who was famous for her contagious laughter.

"It is a pleasure to meet you, Germaine," Aline said and gave her a friendly hug.

Later on, the ladies sang "La Marseillaise" until barrack thirty-one vibrated much to the consternation of the guards outside.

CHAPTER 6

A Worrisome Mistake

Aline was strong, physically and mentally, but there was a limit to her fortitude. In the camp's hostile environment, it had to be only a matter of time when her health would collapse and her mind rendered unable to cope. What rational human could insulate themselves from the intensity of each day's horrors? None of these women could have been prepared for what they endured. The survival instinct was often easier talked about than acted on.

Two months elapsed. Lady X informed her barrack-mates that the Allies were now making fast progress toward Germany, both on the eastern and western fronts. On that news alone, morale went up. But they were not naïve. To be close to Germany was one thing, to be delivered from Ravensbrück was another thing. The battle of Normandy was still raging in many spots and within a few weeks they noticed a drastic increase in the number of incoming prisoners. The resulting pressure on the SS guards drove many to lose the last shreds of their morality. During the early days, the guards' brutality was selectively administrated. Now their wanton depravities—torturing, killing, and cremating people alive—were becoming *de rigueur* throughout the ranks. Ravensbrück was inundated with prisoners. The Nazis' response was to kill faster, more efficiently—the SS were experts on all counts.

One may ask why bother taking prisoners to Ravensbrück if you have to subject them to such misery. Why not kill them when they were taken prisoner? Indeed this was often what was done as this next story illustrates.

My father had two school friends who became electricians. At the time, being an electrician was a high in demand, rewarding job. His friends became involved in the French Resistance and one of them was also a well-known member of the Communist party, which did not help his situation. Their saga began when the Germans raided a communist cell meeting and caught six of its members. They were tortured for days until they gave up the names of their friends, which included my father's friends who were in the French Resistance. Refusing to give up the names of their colleagues in the underground, the Gestapo sent them to the town of Chateaubriand where the Germans arrested men suspected of being anti-German or involved in the Communist party. The Germans captured twenty-seven men of all ages. At the end of the day, the Germans loaded them into trucks and took them to a sand quarry about a mile east of town. Once there, they were brutally off loaded and sprayed with machine gun fire. Survivors were dispatched with a pistol shot to the head. This was one of the most gruesome mass murders in France committed by the Germans except for the infamous Oradour massacre where 642 men, women, and children were similarly abducted and murdered.

After the war, while I was still young, my father would stop and weep every time we passed that quarry. Despite the huge number of people who were murdered or that died in the camps, only a relatively few prisoners of the Nazis made it to the camps. The high proportion of men summarily executed by the Nazis is a mystery to some degree but might make some practical sense as the Germans preferred women as slave laborers in the factories—they were more easily intimidated and malleable. Perhaps this was true at the beginning of the war but I am not sure the logic held toward the end of the war. Obviously the SS and Gestapo were less averse to killing men than women.

Aline had been assigned to the team of prisoners that pushed rail carts filled with ashes from the crematorium to a nearby lake for disposal. When emptied, the rail carts were not too difficult to push, but when they were full of ashes, it was a daunting task. The same carts were used to carry coal from the train to the crematorium. On hot summer days, the black coal dust mixed with perspiration became a terrible irritant for the six days between weekly showers. One summer day, Aline happened to notice that the young woman SS guard watching her, notorious for her meanness, wasn't accompanied by her German Shepherd. As this was very abnormal, Aline slipped-up, took a needed rest, and looked at the guard. The guard saw this and immediately approached Aline, flexing her whip in anticipation of the twenty-five lashes that she was about to administer for Aline's effrontery.

As she raised her whip, Aline stopped pushing the cart and turned to face the guard. Aline glowered, teeth bared, and hands pumping in anticipation of the coming altercation. The guard looked at her face, hands, and powerful wrists. The most intimidating aspect, though, was the wild look in Aline's black eyes. Without the dog, the guard knew she was no match for this woman who had nothing to lose. The guard reached for her gun but Aline stepped forward. The guard knew she would be dead before she could take hold of her gun. Obviously intimidated, the guard turned around and left.

Moments later, the SS woman came back with her dog. Aline knew she was in trouble. Interestingly, the guard did not sic the dog on her. The dog gently put his nose on Aline's foot, an action that meant "don't move." Aline knew she should do nothing as the dog would immediately attack and bite down on her throat. The SS guard came to Aline and pointed her handgun at her head. Aline felt the cold metal. She heard the safety click off and waited for what seemed to be an eternity.

The guard growled, "That would be too easy, bitch! Instead, I am going to destroy you little by little one day at the time."

She ordered the dog to attack Aline's extremities. For five minutes, Aline uselessly struggled with the dog as it savagely bit her feet and her hands. The guard ordered the dog to stop the attack and they walked away. That evening, Aline anguished over the pain caused by the open wounds. Her friends did their best to clean the punctures and deep scratches with the scant water they had. Lady X brought some cotton and cologne to disinfect the wounds as best they could. Aline knew the day's episode with the guard was only the beginning of a long and dangerous adversarial relationship with that German woman, which, most likely, would end with her in the crematorium. She mentally inventoried the extent of damage caused by her mistake, but it was too late.

The next day as Aline took her daily bowl of soup, the SS guard came close to her with the dog and kicked the bowl out of Aline's hands. The soup splashed all over her face and clothes. As meager and unsustaining as their daily ration was, it did provide a basic level of nutrition without which Aline's body would atrophy. Now she would have to go the day without any food. All day, she loaded the cart with human ashes, pushed it to the lake, and unloaded them into the water. Many times she wished she could be among those ashes. She could not help but think of the joy of being released from the guards' hatred and violence, the mutilations from torture, and the hell of surgical experiments. She knew the guard was watching her and she could not afford to make another mistake. She also often pondered whether it would be better to jump on the guard, inflict as much retribution as possible, and let the Nazis end her macabre existence. The dog seemed to read her thoughts, it suddenly growled at her. Aline concentrated on pushing the cart. She glanced at a pile of dead, naked women ready to be sent to the crematorium. This was a common sight she truly hated. At times, some of the women in the pile were not dead but incapable of moving and only moaned.

She saw a robin searching for food among dead leaves and was jealous of those in the outside where they and the songbirds did not have to worry about war or Ravensbrück. This brought her memories back to Petit Louis and the chickadees at home.

"I wonder if someone will open the pump cap for them," she thought. This simple thought gave her courage. Every year, during spring and summer, chickadees would nest in the opened water pump cap. Aline and Louis used the hand-pumped water well for fresh drinking water and water for the garden.

That evening, she collapsed on her bed and wept from pain and pent up anger, hate, and despair. Louisette, Germaine, and Genevieve did their best to comfort her but they knew they would not see Aline for many more days.

One evening, when everyone gathered around Lady X for the latest information on the SS, she said, "The guard who is after Aline is called the Terminator of Ravensbrück. She has a terrible record and is cruelty at its worst."

The next day, Aline went in line for her bowl of soup and her cup of water before reporting to the work team going to the carts. The Terminator was already searching for her. This time, Aline gobbled her soup as fast as possible and drank all of her water. She tried hard to retain her composure and ignore the guard then started her assigned task. She noticed a faint, vicious smile on the Terminator's face. Everything went well until noon then the Terminator's festering hatred boiled over, and she lost her patience waiting for Aline to infract a rule. She and her dog came closer to Aline.

"Work faster, bitch!" she spewed, half German, half French, as she brutally lashed Aline's back five times while Aline tried to shovel the ashes faster.

"You take too few ashes in your shovel!"

Five more lashes landed on Aline's back as she moaned with pain.

Amazed by Aline' resilience, the Terminator relied on her whip even harder and administered five more devastating lashes.

Once the cart was filled, she and another woman pushed it as fast as they could toward the lake.

"You! Don't help that bitch. She can do the pushing all by herself," shouted the Terminator and sent the other woman to another task.

A fully loaded cart required two or three women to push it from the crematorium to the lake. They were never pushed by a lone woman—except today, by Aline. As soon as the ashes were dumped into the lake, she returned to the crematory. Aline was then assigned to unload coal from the train into the little carts under the baleful glare of the Terminator. The coal dust and grit, mixed with the women's perspiration, created an abrasive paste on those hot summer days that acted like sandpaper on the women's skin. Aline was near exhaustion when the Terminator was called to other tasks. Fortunately the replacement guard did not pay undue attention to Aline for the rest of the day. That evening, as Aline lay on her bed, Germaine saw a smile on her face.

"You were lucky today," Germaine said.

"I know, but I wonder where they sent that witch."

Aline never saw the Terminator again. According to the camp's grapevine, she had been promoted and sent to another concentration camp. Aline knew she had to exercise better self-control in the future.

CHAPTER 7

Aline's Anecdote with Genevieve De Gaulle

Aline had learned her lesson. For the next couple of months, she kept a low profile, carefully observing the camp's rules. She followed Germaine's advice, "Be like the ducks, let the water drops run down the feathers. You may shake discretely to make them run down faster, but make sure you are the only one aware of it…"

Aline truly loved Louisette who was always calm and philosophical about their shared fate. Aline's relationships with Genevieve and Germaine Tillion were more elusive. Aline thought both were so well-educated that she felt awkward and intellectually inferior to them (Aline left school at fourteen). Germaine Tillion was young and an anthropologist, but still a kid as far Aline was concerned. Nevertheless she was a very smart and pleasant lady. Yes, these ladies were intimidating; however, they were the type of brilliant souls that France would need to rebuild. Aline knew she would willingly give her life to protect them. Genevieve and Aline transcended their educational gulf with a common love of

songbirds. Genevieve had an almost scientific under-
standing of songbirds' names, habits, and migrating pat-
terns. Aline knew songbirds by watching them at home
with Petit Louis. Their favorite place at home to gently interact with birds was in their garden. With years of
patience, even the timid rouge gorges (a tiny European
robin), chickadees, finches, and merles (common black-
birds) would almost eat from their hands. Without hesitation, the house sparrows ate from their hands.

"At home," Aline said, "Chickadees nested every
year in the water pump's cap in the garden. One year,
we inadvertently left the cap open. The cap was the perfect size for a nest, and very safe about eight feet above
the ground. Somehow Chickadees knew wandering cats
could not climb the heavy cast iron body of the pump.
From then on, every spring we would open the cap for
the waiting chickadees. They would peck at the window,
if needed, to remind us they were back and waiting."
Aline's eyes closed slightly as she looked at her hands
for a few moments.

"This is fascinating!" Genevieve replied.

Aline had recovered reasonably well from the lashes
on her back and dog bites on her lower legs and hands.
There were still a few spots on her right calf that weren't
healing properly.

"The dog bites are in the same place as your varicose
veins," Germaine said, "that is a bad combination. My
mother had the same problem, but without the help of
these stupid dogs."

Aline lay on her bed, her thoughts again drifting to
Petit Louis.

"I hope I will see you again. I don't know what they did to you. I hope you are still alive somewhere. This thought allows me to fight depression. Hope is everything!"

Aline heard through the grapevine that, most likely, Petit Louis had been taken by train to Dachau—the prisoners on that train were rumored to have been subjected to more inhumane conditions than any other, which resulted in many more casualties. Knowing that Petit Louis had been badly tortured and received many serious wounds, Aline was left with scant hope that he survived the horrors of the train. Her intuition was that he died before getting to Dachau. She fought her intuition, hoping it was not accurate. According to French Resistance archives, Louis Virmoux is listed as having died in Dachau.

As Louisette gently massaged Aline's calves, she slowly drifted into a precious, deep sleep.

"Sleep well, my dear friend," Louisette whispered.

Aline had lost a lot of weight. She was still a strong lady but malnutrition had taken its toll. Like most of the prisoners, she had gum disease. All of her teeth were loose. She knew she would lose some of them soon. Yet when she looked at Genevieve and Germaine who had been at the camp much longer, she thought she was lucky in a way. Would any of them make it until they were liberated?

Regularly, the SS came to the camp and formed *Kommandos* (work groups) from the healthier women in the camp. Prisoners selected by *Kapos* were lined up and the SS would select the best for slave labor projects.

Originally, at the beginning of the war, this practice was the true objective of having created Ravensbrück women's camp. So after all there was indeed an economic reason for this place to exist. Kapos were similar to a modern prison trustee in that they were given special privileges in exchange for managing their fellow prisoners. However, they were often recruited from the ranks of violent criminals whose prisoner abuses were overlooked by the SS. Most often, Ravensbrück's Kapos were recruited from Polish women inmates who had arrived during the earliest waves. The women in the Kommandos were barely fed anything and subsisted on meager diets of water and turnips until they ran out of energy and were executed. These ladies who were selected would never come back to Ravensbrück. Fortunately for the French women, the SS favored young Polish women who knew some German.

"You better never talk German again," Aline said several times to Louisette. "I hope that they forgot your offer to translate their orders into French when we arrived."

Germaine Tillion used a risky strategy to avoid working in a Kommando. On the days when Kommandos were formed, she would find any excuse to go to the infirmary by coughing, limping, or sneezing so the SS officer would reject her as a candidate.

"As a good-looking lady," Aline said, "I am amazed how you fooled them so far."

"Aline, do you see my body now? It was you who told me I looked ninety. I am no longer in shape for any kind of hard labor. Actually I have reached the point, after so many problems with my chest, that I don't care if I make it or not."

"Germaine Tillion," Aline said with mock indignity, taking her bony shoulders in her strong hands, "you cannot talk that way. We all need you and I know too well what you have been through. But as long as there is one drop of blood left in your veins, you must continue to fight the bastards. When this shit is over, you will be the best person to relate first person experiences in hell to the world. Your brain is an unbelievable notebook."

Aline's prediction was right on, Germaine would write several books and live to 101.

"Thank you, Aline. You give me courage. You seem indestructible."

"This is a good point," Genevieve replied. "If some of us are liberated, what are we going to do with our lives?"

"I don't know for sure," Aline replied. "I have so much hatred for them that I may fear myself for as long as I live. Don't lecture me. I know perfectly well it is not a good thing to think that way but I cannot help it."

"I think the same way too often," Genevieve replied.

"I often think the same way too," Louisette said.

"I too think the same way," Germaine added.

They all held each other's hands.

Aline continued, "I started feeling intense hatred when they gassed my father and my brother, Emile, during World War I in Verdun. They struggled the rest of their lives until they died of pneumonia at the beginning of World War II. Poor things, they could not take it anymore. This is the main reason I joined Petit Louis in the Resistance. And believe it or not, I hate the Gestapo people even more than the SS themselves."

"I cannot agree more," Genevieve replied passionately.

"In the meantime, ladies, using Aline's words," Germaine said, "all of us are in deep shit!"

They all laughed a little—it was an efficacious and priceless medicine.

"That's my girl!" Aline said, giving Germaine a needed hug.

"Thank you!" Germaine replied, with tears in her eyes.

They all had tears in their eyes as well. Under these stressful circumstances, they developed bonds and priceless friendships. For an instant in their life, that friendship was their only possession. No one could take that away from them, not even the SS.

A few days later, they were called to prepare for the various daily tasks. But this time, the Kapos entered their barrack. They ordered the prisoners to take their personal effects and bedding with them. All the women were rushed out the door. One Kapo locked the door behind them. It was still dark and it happened very fast.

Inside the building, Aline and Genevieve slept deeply. When Genevieve awakened, she looked around, puzzled. She went to the door, worrying she would be late for her assignment, which would get her into big trouble. But the door was locked. This had never happened before when all women were out. She heard someone snoring. It was Aline. She woke her up.

"I think we have a problem," Genevieve said.

"Where is everyone?" Aline asked, yawning.

"That is the point. It is just you and me. They locked the door. We cannot get out."

"You must be kidding!"

They banged on the door. They called. They yelled. They went to the windows. One window was half open behind bars. They called again and again. Tired of trying to get a guard's attention, Aline went to the faucet to wash and get a drink. The water had been turned off as well.

"I don't believe this!"

"This is not good," Genevieve said. "I imagine they locked this barrack for some maintenance, but how long it is going to take before someone comes back?"

All day, they knocked on the door, on windows, and called, and called. But nobody responded to their calls. In fact, they didn't hear anyone outside.

At first they did not worry too much.

The day went by. The night went by. By the end of the next day, they became desperate for water. Fortunately it was raining. Aline and Genevieve took turns cupping their hands outside the window and collected sips of rain to drink. They were at the mercy of the weather. They passed the time by talking about their respective personal lives, families, and friends. Every time they heard a noise outside they would knock on door and windows to attract attention.

At one time, Aline saw a "bergeronette" (white wagtail) building its nest in a small cavity beneath the soffit. They watched the little bird as it continuously wagged its tail while walking on the ground.

"Maybe I should wag like that in front of a Kapo next time!" Aline joked.

They laughed in good humor and resumed talking about birds for half a day. They found that talking about birds was good therapy. It helped purge their minds of their suffering. They heard a crow outside.

"This is the Kapo coming!" Genevieve joked.

Again, they laughed and went to the window to gather rainwater in their hands.

It wasn't until the fifth day of their isolation that someone opened the door, it was a Polish Kapo.

"What are you doing here?" She asked in broken German. "Follow me to the infirmary. You need food and water. Today, you are going to clean and maintain this building."

"We were locked in last week while we slept. And no one roused us when our barrack was emptied," Aline offered.

"I am surprised your absence was not noticed by the Germans," said the Kapo, as she led them to the infirmary.

At the infirmary, a doctor put some cream on the wounds around Aline's calves, which were still not healing.

"Maybe we should get accidentally locked up more often to get better treatment," Genevieve joked.

They were surprised by the Kapo's thoughtfulness. Later on, Genevieve and Aline rejoined their friends in another barrack. They thought Aline and Genevieve had been selected by the SS for Kommando duty.

Aline learned that Louisette had been taken for a Kommando project the day she and Genevieve disappeared.

"We were almost certain you had been taken as well, although we all found it bizarre that nobody noticed," a woman said, adding, "a Kapo told us they had been taken to Schönefeld for heavy airport construction. The Nazis are desperate for cheap labor."

Aline was very sad that her best companion had disappeared.

CHAPTER 8

Aline's New Jobs

When suffering every day, every minute
becomes an eternity, even when you know
the end of the war is coming.

It was bitterly cold in January 1945. Louisette's absence created an unfillable void in Aline's life. She longed to enjoy one more chat with her. Genevieve de Gaulle had also been separated from the group, probably for some political reasons, and most likely isolated in a special cell reserved for very important people. They were told that a top German officer who defected was captured, and placed in one of those cells.

Aline's new jobs were to shovel snow when appropriate, dig trenches when plumbing problems developed, repair rail tracks, and transport bodies to the crematory. She had lost a considerable amount of body weight. Her calf wounds were not doing too badly. The condition of her teeth and gums was disastrous. Only one bottom front tooth remained. She could not chew anything without causing terrible pain from the pressure on her gums. Malnutrition destroyed most women after a few months, Aline was no exception. But what she feared most was the freezing temperatures that could lead to frostbite. Every day during the cold weather, her feet and hands would become fiercely painful then become numb—frostbitten feet would have been a death sentence. Her only relief was at the end of the day, back in her barrack. To protect her hands and feet as best she could, she used an old pair of socks as gloves and wore two pairs of socks to protect her feet. There were not many alternatives. She tried to convince herself that liberation would come soon. They knew from the camp's grapevine the Allies and Russians were simultaneously approaching Germany's western and eastern borders.

Another problem developed that winter, the barracks' plumbing was falling apart. The toilets were over-used and overflowed, forcing many women to relieve themselves outside. To remedy this, long trenches were dug and planks were placed over them so that the women could roost on them, exposing their private parts to everyone.

Of course, the cesspits needed to be occasionally emptied. The honors went to Aline and another French woman once. To visualize the process, imagine a wheelbarrow with the wheel removed and the handles extended so two people could carry the barrow between them. Now, you have a twenty-five-gallon handbarrow that could be used to carry the cesspit waste to the camp's gardens. After slopping the handbarrow full, the women would lug their malodorous "treasure" to the gardens, which were about a quarter mile away. The camp's gardens were used to grow potatoes, turnips, and rutabagas that were fed to the prisoners.

The SS guards insisted that each handbarrow must be completely filled before being taken to the gardens. The guards' innate perversity found humor when the two-woman teams struggled with their loads to the gardens. Any slip or falter as they walked rewarded them with handbarrow's contents sloshed and splashed on their legs, shoes, socks, and clothes while the guards laughed and laughed. It was cheap entertainment. Fortunately when they reached the gardens, the SS guard in charge was a nice, relatively considerate person. He guided them to where their load should be dumped.

Aline and her companion looked enviously at some of the remaining late winter vegetables.

"Maybe we will have a few potato peelings in the soup tomorrow morning," Aline said.

"Don't talk when you are working," the guard snapped.

"I need to shit," Aline's partner said.

"Go in your clothes," the guard replied. "Move on and shut up! You know that you can't relieve yourself when you're at work and, remember, I am the gentle guard."

What the guard said was true and they both knew better from past experience. As for Aline, one of the hardest parts of contending with the frigid weather was the bad shoes—not really a shoe but a cheap sandal that did not provide good traction in snow, mud, and dirt. Frostbite was always a big concern during the winter. Wooden shoes were a luxury for a few privileged prisoners.

At the end of the day, when both women went back to the barrack they were given plenty of space, as they looked and smelled like shit. It was nearly impossible to get enough water to clean their bodies and clothes after cesspit duty. Worse yet, it was especially difficult to dry clothes before next morning's call for work.

The next morning Aline commented, "I never moved so much shit in my entire life even when I was a teen mucking out the nearby farm's cow barns. But I don't mind as someone has to do it. I would love to dump the damn Boche SS in the pit, but I guess this is a pleasure I will never have."

She and her friends laughed at the thought of an SS guard in the cesspit.

"Actually," said Aline, "I had a little pleasure yesterday. I saw some blackhead chickadees in the garden pecking at some leftover sunflowers. The sight instantly took my mind off the stupid SS guard. At home, I have blue-headed chickadees. Petit Louis and I love them."

Germaine took her hand and embraced her dear comrade.

"You are something else, lady! Sometimes I think your mind is indestructible."

"Oh no! My mind has its limits, believe me," Aline answered, tearing up.

Others joined them and they started retelling old stories they all knew by heart. They knew the war was coming to an end, but every minute had become its own eternity for these women. They had very little energy left. Still, they found the energy to sing the French national anthem, La Marseillaise.

Aline was assigned to the cesspit for a full week, at the end of which she was again ordered to push carts filled with human ashes from the crematory to the nearby lake. At the end of the day, back in her barrack, she started a friendly relationship with a new American prisoner named Virginia who taught her some English.

Always trying to find a bright spot in life, Aline was thankful she never had to push the massive rollers to level trails and streets. This was a punishment for those condemned to die soon. Being assigned to a roller was the last job a prisoner would do, it nearly always ended in death. Once more, she thought she had been very lucky for the Terminator to be transferred just at the right time.

CHAPTER 9

From Ravensbrück to Schönefeld

Aline, now a living skeleton, started to pray for
God's help—something she rarely did. That action
alone told her she had reached her limits.

During February and March 1945, Ravensbrück
overseers started to worry about the war's course. It
was becoming increasingly evident Germany would lose
the war very soon. As a result, the SS began to method-
ically eliminate women in poor health so the SS would
not look too bad on judgment day. Every day, guards
would go to the barracks and select women they con-
sidered as being in poor health then one or two trucks
would stop at the barracks and the selected women were
loaded. The SS's selection criteria seemed to be based
on bad legs, bad lungs, the way they walked, high fever,
and so forth. It was becoming very difficult to hide ill
friends. Whenever the prisoners walked about the yard
or performed their tasks, the SS observed them carefully
and noted who looked ill, these lists were passed to their
superiors. According to Aline, because her job was to
empty railroad carts filled with human ashes into the lake,
she estimated that between 150 and two hundred women

were exterminated daily. Women who resisted were shot on site and thrown into the trucks like a bag of potatoes. Some women were so ill the guards did not even bother to kill them before sending them to the crematory, that is, after their clothes had been removed. Every day, Aline's health and energy levels dropped. She was continually tired. It took all of her energy to stand. She wondered how long it would take before they selected her. Despite her physical degradation, her strong mind gave her the appearance of being strong and still capable of doing hard work.

But around the middle of March 1945, several hundred women were selected to go to an unspecified outside Kommando. Aline was one of them. An important clue led them to believe they were not being sent for extermination or, at least, not yet. The clue being that the SS was careful to select only strong and relatively healthy women. Obviously, they were needed somewhere for heavy labor—as expendable slaves. They were packed into the all too familiar railroad cattle cars. The trip was slow, but not too long. When the train stopped and the guards opened the car, Aline saw many construction projects: roads, buildings, runways, power lines, and trenches everywhere. Thousands of women and men worked hard using their bare hands. Someone familiar with the area, a Polish woman, told them they were South of Berlin not too far from Schönefeld.

Aline was again assigned to push little railroad carts. This time, they were full of concrete ready to be poured. As such, the carts were considerably heavier than those full of human ashes but at least two or sometimes three women were assigned per cart. A benefit of this task was that they were provided with plenty of water to drink and more food than usual. Obviously, they wanted to keep these workers in good shape for as long as they were needed.

The first night in the barrack, Aline realized that several hundred women here were a mix of Poles, German outcasts, Czechs, Russians, Ukrainians, Gypsies, and a few French women (who snubbed her). Finding little in common with any of her fellow prisoners, she regretted being separated from her comrades at Ravensbrück, however, at least, she was relatively well-fed.

After a few days, Aline's strength noticeably improved. She observed her surroundings. She noted that although the area was heavily guarded, it was not heavily fenced like Ravensbrück. She started fostering the notion of escaping. Being in the center of Germany, almost anyone would have said escape was an insane idea. But at night, when everything was silent besides a few couples making love, she could hear artillery fire coming from the distant southwest and east. The proximity of the Allies to central Germany so close to Berlin meant the end of the war was coming. The thought bolstered her morale and gave credence to her thoughts of escaping. She reasoned that if she had an opportunity she would go southwest where, she guessed, the Germans were fighting Americans and British divisions. She knew that walking through a battlefront would be suicidal. At this point, she did not care but decided to be prudently patient.

One night, the thumping of artillery fire mixed with the thunder of a lightning storm toward the east created a majestic concert that thrilled Aline and lifted her spirits. She had a rough day, her ankles and calves were agonizingly painful especially the right side, which never completely healed from the bites inflicted by the Ravensbrück German Shepherds. Earlier that day, she witnessed the SS guards executing several exhausted women who could not handle the work anymore. Knowing the penalty for not being able to perform, women would push themselves to look able but then collapse from the effort. These, too, were killed without mercy and tossed into trucks that took them somewhere—to crematories? To mass graves? SS cruelty could not and cannot be described with words. It was and is mind-boggling that so-called humans could do such horrific things to their fellow humans.

"Bastard Boches!" Aline murmured to herself many times that day.

"It was the way they would throw them in the truck like a bag of potatoes even when they were still alive and wounded," Aline told me many times with tears in her eyes. "They would eventually die denied of any remote form of dignity as, at long last, they reached the point where death was a welcome deliverance. The SS killers were devoid of consciences that could harbor even a spark of guilt."

CHAPTER 10

Aline's Escape

An inner light told Aline her day was coming. Yes, she would find the necessary energy.

The following may not be absolutely accurate, as Aline's memory of some details was not at its best. It is the general thrust that counts as her actions were astonishing acts of courage.

Early one morning, a group of French women were selected to be transferred to the Red Cross and were lined up in front of trucks. Then the quiet was shattered by exploding artillery shells or from an aerial bombardment by the Allies or both. A great deal of confusion ensued as some women were told to get in the trucks and others to run to a shelter. The German soldiers ran to underground shelters and let the prisoners fend for themselves. Aline saw a nearby gate that was left wide open. She knew trying to escape was certain death on a normal day. But this was not a normal day. It was clear that Soviet troops were approaching. Her instinct told her to get out. Several other women told her to remain with the group.

"The liberation has arrived, so don't do anything funny you would regret," a French woman told her.

"You know, ladies, I have been through hell for ten months, and frankly I don't care anymore if I make it or not. Basically, I am already gone."

She ran through the gate and saw German soldiers dead nearby a truck. Artillery rounds blasted the area. Aline ran as fast as she could. She took a coat from a dead soldier then looked at his boots, they were about the right size. She tried one on and it felt good. Nearby, a Soviet soldier slumped, near death, still holding his machine gun. Being familiar with machine guns of all types from her training in the French Resistance, she grabbed the heavy gun. Because of her diminished physical condition, it felt much heavier than she remembered. She noticed the magazine was full. The dying Soviet soldier pointed to a German soldier coming in their direction. Aline instantly opened fire, one bullet straight to his head. "Folks, from now on, I am in charge of my destiny!"

Out of the corner of her eyes, Aline saw some men and women running away. She guessed they were going in the opposite direction from the troops coming from the east. She guessed they were Soviet troops. She went due west to where she could see and hear the heavy artillery battle going on. She guessed it was from the American front, which she liked better. Events were taking place very fast and there was not much time to think.

She walked along small deserted roads for several hours. It was early morning and the sun had risen. She trudged on in a fine but chilling mist. She was thankful for the German coat she wore over her shabby prison clothes. At this stage she was full of adrenaline, fighting for survival. However, her strength flagged and her mind was becoming fuzzy. It was difficult to focus because of her hunger, thirst, and fatigue.

She instinctively walked near or under bushes and shrubs. At one point, Aline's fatigue got the best of her. She fell to the ground and took a little nap. At this point, she barely knew the difference between reality and a dream. She was awakened by robins looking for food under the dead leaves.

"If the birds are safe, I am safe!" she murmured and went back to sleep until about midday.

CHAPTER 11

Aline's Journey to Freedom

Walking free in a forest gave her the will to keep going. In a forest, she was in her element.

Aline came upon a lake and followed its northern shore and proceeded west, walking through a hamlet. She saw an old man going to his home with a loaf of bread and a pot that might contain milk. She went to him and pointed the machine gun at his chest, motioning toward the bread and milk. The man did not resist, realizing Aline's fierce determination. Later on, she changed directions worrying that the man might inform on her and give her whereabouts to the Germans. She carefully walked on grass to prevent making obvious tracks. She trudged southwesterly along a dirt trail that probably led to a farm, she was not sure. Her only reference was the heavy artillery firing far ahead of her. She was convinced it was the American/German battle line.

"My English is terrible!" she murmured to herself. "How am I going to explain the German coat and the Russian machine gun?"

She smiled and decided to worry about this later. She saw a few buildings ahead so she headed south and entered a forest. Now she was worried that German troops might be hiding in the forest. She was thirsty and sipped from the pot immediately realizing the pot contained water and not milk—she was pleased that it was water as milk would have been too rich for her condition. All day, she carefully traveled through woods and meadows, never seeing a soul. She decided to change course slightly and head southwesterly where the distant rumbling of artillery sounded like a never-ending thunderstorm. She reached the edge of the forest that provided a panoramic view of a valley and the battlefront. It was late in the afternoon and she was exhausted. She decided to sleep at the forest's fringe under the shelter of heavy shrubs. She ate some bread and threw away the crust that she could not chew much to the delight of a nearby squirrel.

"You don't care about this war, little thing. You are lucky to be what you are!" she whispered.

Before dusk, she noticed a tiny robin hopping near her feet.

She sipped some water. If her distress from the festering dog bites weren't enough, Aline struggled with diarrhea, which had been a chronic problem for her since she was incarcerated. While in the camps, she managed to secure a few activated charcoal tablets from the infirmary to help combat the problem. Now she had only two tablets left, which she swallowed. She was aware that eating too much bread too quickly would make her sick, so she rationed herself to small nibbles every two hours. Getting ready to sleep, she covered herself with as many dead leaves as she could. The thick layer of dead leaves protected under shrubs made the best bed she had for ten months. She kept her hand on the machine gun that she had hidden under the leaves and fell into a deep sleep.

She was abruptly awakened at dawn by the sound of artillery and heavy military vehicles clanking through the forest. She skulked to the edge of the forest where she heard some German soldiers talking. She carefully crept back to a very large oak tree near the shrubs where she slept, which provided protection from being run over by tanks. Again she covered herself with dead leaves, keeping her fingers on the machine gun. One German soldier stopped near the edge of the forest and relieved his bladder while talking to another soldier farther away.

"If they see me, they're both dead. Of course I would be killed but it would be two for one, therefore I win," Aline reasoned.

After a while, the soldiers and tanks went away. She waited for about fifteen minutes before carefully making her way to the forest's edge where she had a better view of her surroundings. On the north, she could see a hornet's nest of troops and tanks through a stand of trees. As there appeared to be no activity to the south, she decided to hug the edge of the forest and walk in that direction. She noticed a river at the bottom of a nearby valley. Meanwhile, the tempo of artillery rounds being exchanged across the river increased.

"The Americans are on the other side of the river," she murmured. "But their guns are overshooting the German line."

With extreme caution, she clambered down an embankment and approached the river wondering how she could cross it. Crossing via a bridge was a poor idea as they would be watched by both sides. Using a small abandoned fishing boat tethered to a tree was also not an option, as it would be immediately seen by both sides. She knew she would have to swim across.

She undressed under a willow and packed her shabby clothes, shoes, and socks inside the German coat. Before crossing, she noticed a few morels growing on the ground. She smiled and said, "Petit Louis would have loved them!" Memories and reflections like these were essential to bolstering her energy and mental health. They were enough to generate sufficient adrenaline to cope with her terrible situation.

She tied the clothing bundle to the machine gun's muzzle, held it over her head, and waded into the water, trying to keep her clothes as far above her head as possible without becoming a target. Although the water was freezing cold, the adrenaline and her drive kept her going as she treaded water and swam diagonally across and downstream. The river was not very wide, and within a short time, she reached the other shore and climbed through high reeds that hid her. Continuing up the river's bank, she came across a large stand of hazelnut trees that provided good cover. Taking her time, she dried off and put her clothes on.

"Aline," she thought, "perhaps wearing a German soldier's coat and boots might not be a good idea when approaching the American line."

She decided to abandon the coat but kept the boots and Soviet machine gun. Once clothed, she left the riverside and followed the thick vegetation that separated last year's wheat fields.

While walking under the hazelnut trees, she glanced down and saw a few blewit mushrooms growing. Being larger than her hands, she thought, "Petit Louis would have gone crazy about those. When we get home, we will go to the forest right away to collect mushrooms."

Not far ahead, German artillery shells pounded the American line. She knew she was very close to the Americans now. Despite having some shells fall near her, she had no fear of dying. She proceeded as if nothing was happening. Concussions from the blasts were enough to cause some hearing loss. To minimize further damage, she pulled her clothes over her head and kept plodding. Her memories from this moment forward would stay with her until the day she died.

CHAPTER 12

Rescued

Seeing an Allied soldier was an immense pleasure, and, yes, she could have given her life to save that soldier.

A line walked cautiously from tree to tree. A few artillery shells fell close by, sending shockwaves through her body. She was at the wrong place at the wrong time. A nearby moan startled her, making her fall to the ground, her hands on the machine gun. Looking around, she saw two dead American soldiers about fifty feet in front of her. Another sat on the ground, visibly injured. Apparently, he could not walk on his own.

"These are American soldiers who walked through artillery fire," Aline murmured to herself. "Perhaps they were on a reconnaissance mission. I cannot abandon the wounded one."

She walked to the wounded soldier who looked at her and wondered if he was hallucinating. Confused by seeing this toothless, bedraggled woman who looked a hundred years old and wore tattered clothes, he reached for his gun. Aline's commanding gesture and her gentle smile convinced him to stop.

"I am a French prisoner of war and I just escaped from the camp where I was a slave worker," Aline said in broken English.

He looked at her again in disbelief and wondered what to do. She turned and raised her blouse, showing him the deep scars and welts on her back. This convinced him she was telling the truth.

She sat close to him and asked about his wound.

"It is my leg… I think I have a broken ankle."

"Let me see it," she said raising his pant leg.

He pointed at the Soviet machine gun.

"How did you get that thing?"

"It is a long story. During my escape, I met a wounded Soviet soldier. He told me to take it, or I think that is what he said. He had no more than a few minutes to live. Anyway, he was in a much worse condition than you, kid. But you have other wounds on your back, don't you?"

"Yes," he replied, "some shrapnel hit me. The larger pieces killed my friends. Fortunately, I was ahead of them."

He took her hand, "Lady, you should go. My unit is not far away."

Aline sat calmly near him and looked him straight in the eyes. He found strange strength in her dark eyes. Somehow he knew she was a no-nonsense woman that would do exactly as she pleased.

"My name is Aline, and I am an officer of the French Resistance. I know I look like hell! What is your name?"

"I am Sergeant X"

After researching old wartime archives about this event for which Aline was decorated by the Americans with the Medal of Freedom, I did not find any record of the event or the soldier's name. Aline told me he was a sergeant. I vaguely recall her saying his name was Ray, but I am not sure. Also, she told me that story so many times without any variation that it is impossible for it not to be true. The Medal of Freedom was also awarded to her past Resistance activities with Petit Louis.

"Sergeant X," she said with an authoritarian voice and a sad smile on her face, "listen to me very good, kid! I went through hell for the last ten months and I am not ready to leave you anytime soon. Either we both make it or neither of us will make it. Is this clear?"

"Yes, Madam!" he replied, admiring the woman's energy despite her terrible condition. Her behavior was irresistible.

She took his knife and cut four branches from a hazelnut tree. She removed the shoots and leaves, creating four sticks about three-quarters of an inch in diameter and about two feet long. She cut a few strips from her shabby prison clothes and firmly tied the branches to his leg. While she ministered to him, he glimpsed the scars on her legs and back.

"At one point you were in worse shape than me."

She did not answer but shook her head with a smile. He thought she had a beautiful smile and because of her ministrations, he knew he would survive and was immensely thankful.

"If I help you, can you get up with your good leg?"

It took Sergeant X two tries, but he succeeded.

"Keep one arm around my neck and hold your machine gun with your other hand... Yes, like that! You can also use the gun as a cane. Now, kid, you know the way better than I do."

Aline abandoned the Soviet machine gun to better help him. Half an hour later and being barely missed by more artillery shells, Aline saw some activity ahead of them. Seeing Aline helping the hobbling sergeant, two soldiers came to help. When they saw this skeleton of a woman in terrible condition holding their companion, they looked at one another in disbelief. Aline let them take over and she followed them as best she could. She was completely exhausted and could not take it anymore. She saw two other soldiers come to her rescue. She was taken to a nearby truck and driven back to their unit where she met an American colonel. In tears, she briefly introduced herself and related her story.

The American colonel exchanged a few words with his medical staff and a doctor came to Aline.

"You are physically destroyed," the young doctor said. "What bothers you most?"

"A lot of things, kid," Aline chuckled. "I have dysentery, bites from German Shepherds on my legs that don't heal, I have many cuts in my back that are infected. You name it and I have it!"

The military doctor opened her shabby clothes and showed her back to the colonel who was visibly shocked. They both shook their heads in disbelief wondering what kind of person could endure such physical battering and who could have committed such brutality on a defenseless woman.

The doctor looked at her legs, especially her right leg, "We better take care of that one soon. It is potential for gangrene."

"What you did today, in your condition, is one of the bravest and most heroic acts I ever seen, lady," the colonel said. Turning to a younger officer, he continued, "I want that woman well-taken care of and I want her name recorded for her later recovery and in due time, her honors. She should be an inspiration for our soldiers."

The colonel came back to Aline.

"Aline is your name."

"Yes, sir!"

"You were on the other side of the river not long ago."

"Yes, sir!"

"What did you see? My reconnaissance men did not make it as you well know."

"Give me a map," Aline asked, "and I will show you where the bastards are. For one thing, your artillery was landing too far away."

As the medics gave her urgent necessary attention, she pointed to where the German troops were concentrated in the forest.

"They have artillery, but I can assure you there are a lot of troops and tanks as well."

"This is very valuable information," the colonel said. "Redirected artillery and a squadron of P-38 aircraft may help us."

He had a smile on his face and this was the last time she saw him.

Two days later, she was reunited with some French prisoners who had been liberated by the Red Cross in Schönefeld. She briefly met Louisette for the last time.

For Charlotte Aline Virmoux, the war was over. In a few days, she was back in France When she was escorted to the American hospital near Paris in April 1945. She weighed only ninety pounds, compared to the 160 pounds she weighed before her capture in April 1944.

On January 18, 1947, 33 Rue du Faubourg Saint Honoré in Paris at the American Embassy, the Supreme Commander of American Forces in Europe (very likely but not completely sure, it may have been a subordinate) Major General Dwight D. Eisenhower delivered the Medal of Freedom to Lieutenant Charlotte Aline Virmoux for her exceptional services. During that ceremony, the brave warrior, Aline, could not control her tears.

CHAPTER 13

A Long Recovery

Posttraumatic disorder was common for many people those days though the majority did not care as they were safe and life was returning to normal… Maybe!

For the next six months, Aline had excellent medical attention at an American hospital near Paris. She always praised the staff for taking care of her as though she was part of their family. As far as I can remember, my great-aunt had immense respect for the Americans and what they went through liberating Europe from the evil of a mad man and his minions. I personally saw her passionately defend America's actions, which did not always go well with some of her friends, family members, or other French audiences.

After she regained some muscle mass and got acquainted with her false teeth, she was a good looking woman again for her age and what she had gone through.

But there was something nobody could help her with at the time: memories. Her memories couldn't be turned off, they haunted her during the day, in bed at night, and when she was alone. She always answered the doorbell with a loaded shotgun. She slept with a loaded shotgun next to her in the bed. When alone at home, she sat in the living room for hours incapable of concentrating on anything. She feared to be alone. When she talked to her dog, the dog intuitively listened sensing its importance to its mistress. The dog often made attempts to respond and share its love with Aline. She did the same with birds in her garden. Aline would even talk to trees and mushrooms in the forest. At times she felt guilty for having survived. She also had a sense of uselessness after the war. It was as though someone said, "Retire, take your pension, and be happy with that." The presence of friends and family was a blessing that liberated her mind from depression and sense of irrelevancy. Her posttraumatic stress disorder was a battle she had to fight on her own. Indeed at the time, nobody paid much attention to psychological wounds only to physical wounds.

Permanent wounds to one's mind was almost taken as a curse, something for which the person should be ashamed. From my close relationship with her, I remember many revealing details that she told me while struggling with unimaginably dark memories everyday of her life. By nature, she was a fighter and not a negative person. However there was absolutely nothing that could erase the memories of Ravensbrück. She constantly had the fear that someone would attack her, often leading to odd behaviors that others didn't understand. She clashed with my mother, who suffered from bouts of bad temper, to the point that Aline would visualize my mother as a Kapo when they argued. As a result, in 1949, my mother completely turned her back on Aline and cast their relationship aside. From that day forward I saw my great-aunt only when I visited her with my grandparents.

Every year, because my grandfather worked for the railroad that we would travel for free, they took me to their home for a summer vacation during July and August. We would always stay a few days with Aline and sometimes she would come to their place for a few weeks. I recall that these visits brought happiness to her face. She was a fun person to be with, always, and she never complained about her condition. When I was a student in Paris, I visited her and never told my mother about it. Aline told me several times I was a peaceful boy and she always found peace of mind when talking to or observing me. I took this as a compliment and perhaps it made me more aware of the importance of peace in our lives. Many times the media came to her home and asked questions about Ravensbrück. They offered her a lot of money if she was willing to reminisce. She always refused to discuss her experiences with the media. She could talk to us because it was in her terms. I quickly learned that it was a bad idea to ask her questions, though. When asked questions, her brain would seize somewhat as a self-defense mechanism. During those episodes, she was incapable of properly connecting to her inner feel-ings—the connection had to be self-initiated. It had to be natural. Many times she told me, "There are memories I will never share with anyone, even you!" In other words, horrors described in this memoir are only the tip of the iceberg of things we will never know.

I was well aware of her mental struggle as I had my own posttraumatic stress disorder when I was a child.

Mine started during the bombings at Normandy and the frequent low altitude attacks from American P-38 Lightning aircrafts. It was exacerbated while we were at my grandparents during 1944–1945 and I witnessed the devastation from the bombings and shelling. These events had devastating effects on a young brain. The sound of air raid sirens' wailing as we ran to the basements of friendly neighbors fearing for our lives often triggered my PTSD. After the "all clear," we would walk to town and see the carnage. Until I was about ten, I had an uncontrollable fear of planes. Even at home, the sound of a plane sent me scrambling under the nearest table. As a conditioned reflex, I did this once in school making all my friends laugh at me. It was only in 1952, when my parents moved to Nice in southern France, that my fear started to dissipate mainly because we lived close to the airport. The sight of many commercial aircraft taking off and landing several times a day finally cured me.

And I wasn't the only one with posttraumatic stress disorder problems. Even our cat, Sapho, didn't escape the war's traumatizing effects. I remember that every time Sapho heard a plane, her tail would triple in volume and she'd dash for shelter. Actually, I recall that Sapho heard the planes long before we did.

My mother's older sister and her husband who lived in Flers, south of where I was born, lost everything during the bombings. They never recovered and were deeply depressed, suffering from significant hearing losses and having nowhere to go. They finished their lives as alcoholics. Sadly, they too were cast aside by my mother this time because they wouldn't listen to her advice. The spillover from their problems was so severe that it often triggered fights between my mother and father.

Another case of posttraumatic stress disorder in my family was my mother's father. He spent four years in the trenches during WW I. When his four-year-old son died from meningitis in 1917, my grandfather was sent home from the battlefront for the funeral. A week later when he returned to the front, he found that his battalion had been wiped out and he was the only survivor. For the rest of his life, he fought the guilt of having abandoned his comrades. The fact that he had been gassed added to his despair.

Following my long battle with pneumonia at age five, my parents were told by our family doctor to take me to the Brittany seashore during July and August where I could recover by breathing the iodized ocean air. My parents called my grandparents to take care of the business at our village (a coffee/bar, the post office, and a grocery store). After one month, my grandparents joined us in Brittany and my great-aunt, Aline, took care of the business for another month.

We had a half-grown pig at the time named Kiki. Every day, Aline fed Kiki with boiled potatoes or other leftover food.

"You are a spoiled piglet! I wish we had such good food in Ravensbrück. You better not complain, kid."

One day, she did not close the gate properly as she ran to the house when someone called her from the post office.

"Okay, okay, I am coming!" she said.

While Aline was at the post office, Kiki opened the door with his nose and escaped to the village. This took place early in the morning before work when most people started socializing in the main street and preparing for a busy day. Aline ran after the pig, wearing only a light, transparent nightgown. She finally caught Kiki and took the 160-pound pig in her arms. The entire village was watching in the street and from their windows, some laughing and some scandalized by her outfit. It sure was the day's entertainment.

"What?" she asked. "You never saw a half-naked woman! These people have no idea what we went through in the concentration camp."

Some men were very impressed by her carrying a 160-pound pig, knowing very well they could not do it themselves. Standing close to the village mayor and the priest who was laughing until tears rolled down his cheeks, a young man made a joke about Aline and the pig.

Aline walked up to him and pointed the pig's nose at his chest.

"Be careful, boy, I may kick your plumbing!"

"Don't mess up with the lady," the mayor told the young man. The priest could not stop laughing.

Aline went home and put Kiki back into its pen.

"Don't do that again, four-legged fat boy, or I will make sausage out of you!"

She went back to the post office where a farmer was still waiting for her.

"What can I do for you sir?" she asked.

"Call the veterinarian. The cow is sick!" he responded.

She checked the list of important telephone numbers prepared by my father and dialed the number then handed the phone to the farmer.

"Sir, come now, the cow is sick." Then the man hung up the phone.

Aline laughed at him.

"Don't you think you should have given him your name and address?"

"How do I know this stuff?"

Aline shook her head and called the veterinarian back and gave him instructions. Then she looked outside the window. Everyone in the village was still chatting about the incident with the piglet.

After making a massive impression on the villagers, Aline was the object of many stories and jokes for a long time—although everyone respected her and liked her for adding some excitement to their boring days. She was especially patient when telling her concentration camp stories to the old veterans of World War I, especially two brothers. One had a wooden leg, the other was missing an arm. Several of the veterans had been gassed just like her brother, Emile. They soon reached the point when the old veterans returned to the café everyday to chat with her. They were her new friends and it was good therapy for them and Aline. It was obvious that many of them never recovered from posttraumatic stress disorder resulting from the horrors of trench warfare and the devastating artillery assaults. Like the casualties from WWII, these forgotten WWI warriors were desperate for psychological healing—alas, nobody cared. They were supposed to be happy with their meager government pension and go away.

When we returned to the village of Forcé, Aline and my grandparents stayed with us for another three weeks. One afternoon, Hans, one of the two German prisoners who worked in the orchards at the neighboring castle, came to the grocery store to buy cigarettes and matches. Although both ex-prisoners could have been repatriated, they decided to stay in France much to the profound and deep resentment of the villagers. Reasons were not clear but because they were from the part of Germany occupied by Soviet forces, they were not in hurry to take another risk at their fate, at least not yet.

When Aline saw him coming toward the store, she said: "I cannot serve that bastard, or I will kill him with my bare hands."

"The war was not his fault," my father argued. Meanwhile, my mother served him. To further assuage Aline's ire, my father told her the mushroom story of when Hans explained the differences between good Agaricus and poisonous Amanita mushrooms to me.

Two weeks later, Hans returned to the store to buy cigarettes and drink beer at the bar with his companion. But only Hans could speak a little French. This time, Aline served him and exchanged a few words. Hans told her he was a soldier of the Wehrmacht and admired Field Marshal Erwin Rommel who was forced to commit suicide by ingesting cyanide pills for conspiring against Hitler and end the war earlier. Then he showed her a picture of his wife and two children.

"Nice family!" Aline said.

"I did not see them for four years, but we exchange mail."

"It is my guess you will see them soon. By the way, I know the difference between the Wehrmacht and the SS very well."

That day when I was five, I listened to the conversation between Aline and Hans. Even now, I vividly recall the details. During that chat, Aline briefly explained her journey to Ravensbrück. Hans seemed fascinated and sad.

She went back to the grocery store for a minute and came back with two packs of cigarettes and said, "This is on me, kid!"

Then she left for the post office.

As I mentioned, even years later, I can recall that conversation as though it took place yesterday. I am amazed that little snippets of life can make such an indelible impression on people's minds. In my case, it took me until adulthood before I fully understood its importance. I have recalled that incident many times when reading the Bible in church or listening to the priest during a Sunday sermon. I am humbled and very impressed that an action like Aline's can be a better teacher than a thousand lectures on compassion and magnanimity.

Back at her home, south of Paris, Aline had a full-time job in a delicatessen only a few blocks away from her house that was run by a close friend of Petit Louis.

On several occasions while I was a teen, I visited her with my grandparents. She and I always went to the forest to collect mushrooms. I recall being concerned about how to determine which mushroom is good and the other bad. She smiled and said her criterion is, "Petit Louis liked that one, Petit Louis did not like that one."

This convinced me that if I wanted to live a long and healthy life, I better find a good book and educate myself about mushrooms. And this is what I did!

The last time I visited Aline was during July 1965, a few days before she passed away from wounds on one of her legs that had not healed and became gangrenous, the lingering result of the dog bites inflicted, an aftermath from the heavy wounds endured at Ravensbrück. Two months later, she would have been seventy.

EPILOGUE

"Many of us should be persuaded to abandon our differences, ignore the other fellow's naivety and shallowness, look at bizarre ideas, and begin to do what has been done before by wise long-forgotten men and women, and what must and will be done sooner or later. Withdraw from the swamp we are in and search for the correct upstream tributary of the river, one that leads to the source we all seek."
—Charles Oliver Ingamells, a good friend of mine

I started writing this epilogue several years ago while I wrote my other novels *Heirs of a Lost Race* and *Rapa-Nui Settlers* as well as several technical and scientific books. You may rightly wonder what connects exploring Polynesians, technical and scientific topics, and a story that took place at the Ravensbrück concentration camp during World War II.

Ever since I was first told Aline's story by my relatives and, especially, by my great-aunt, Aline, I have wondered how we humans can learn the ultimate lesson—that is to ensure that such devastating historical events are not repeated. For some time I thought the world might have learned its lesson, especially at the end of the Cold War and when the Berlin wall was brought down—suddenly there was hope. But September 11, 2001, and the continuing rise of terrorism changed my views. I became convinced that we humans (or *Homo sapiens*, I should say) have a serious problem to resolve because conflict is the rule, and peace the exception. As a result, it was my choice to elevate this epilogue to a far higher level than the horrors of Ravensbrück. As better books than this have been written by firsthand on-site witnesses. What are the logical lessons, conclusions, and recommendations we could learn from such a disturbing story and the many others that continue to unfold today?

In my opinion, the answer may be found in Aristotle's ancient philosophy, which was reinvented and practiced by ancient Polynesians: *Who we are is irrelevant. What counts is who we want to be.*

If we had followed this philosophy during the last two millennia, infamous conquests, the Crusades, the Holocaust, Ravensbrück, World War I, World War II, the Cold War, September 11, 2001, and this cancer we call terrorism would have been greatly mitigated or never existed. All of these plagues on humanity happened because we were taught to be thralls, easy prey for rulers to use and manipulate as they wished. This devious, well-planned, subtle, and ruthlessly implemented ideology has been responsible for the unnecessary death and suffering of many hundreds of millions of people over the millennia. Furthermore, we are still affected by this primitive instinct leading to bursts of rage much too often and we still don't know how to cure such disastrous brain circuitry shortcomings. Basically the more arrogant the winner is, the more in rage the loser becomes. We better be careful about this as it is leading to a very dangerous vicious circle.

It is time to stop this nonsense if we intend to survive and, one day, travel beyond the small blue dot called Earth. Even in our democracies today, we can sense the quest for power from many talented (but misdirected) people. It has become a viral obsession.

To analyze this issue properly, we need to step back and take a deep, objective look at ourselves and abandon our perception of who we think we are and embrace who we really are. Introspection is easier said than done as very few people have the enlightenment or discipline to selflessly search for something as ethereal and remote from our day-to-day lives. Albert Einstein once said inspirationally, "There is something in each of us that nobody knows."

This is an enlightened and formidable statement and, yes, it is in us and it is big. It is too bad we don't praise Einstein more for his insightfulness. In my opinion, he was not only a superb scientist but a formidable philosopher and peacemaker as well—and a German! Remember, this epilogue transcends the horrors of Ravensbrück, which is only one example among many. This epilogue hopes to elevate the debate about what can be done—if, and only if, we can make up our minds to create and embrace a new vision.

Let's look at the way we prevent conflicts today as our erroneous conventional wisdom guides us. By trusting that deterrence is the best strategy, as we do, it is only a matter of time before a fatal error, misjudgment, or crazed mind affected by uncontrollable rage will "pull the trigger" and send civilization to its inevitable end. Of this, I am very sure.

So who are we? It is important to answer this question. And, dear friend, the answer isn't found in the rhetoric spewed by tyrants and governments for millennia. The answer is far subtler.

Let's keep the lessons of Ravensbrück in mind as we explore the numerous times God has shown us the proper path to follow. As history has proven, humans don't know how to read or interpret the divine words given to us over thousands of years. As one of many examples, God said to Moses, "I am that I am." Jesus said, "I am the light of the world."

The power and simplicity of these messages are amazing. God is our true identity—we are part of God. There is no such thing as God and us, therefore we should never be ashamed of who we are. The Bible, like other well-known historical documents, was written by well-educated scribes who served intelligent rulers. Very often, revealed wisdom and divine messages are only metaphors. They guide us to what we should do and should not do, and that is all. But many people take words literally, which is not always the right thing to do or the intent of the author. The Supreme Being and divinities such as Abraham, Moses, Jesus Christ, prophets, Buddha, Ra, Make Make, Taaroa, Virgin Mary, and others are like holographic manifestations created to guide us, nudge us, and then wait for the results. By definition, if these holograms were created by a Universal Consciousness, they are positive influences that promote peace, creativity, and harmony.

It is sadly comical when "enlightened" scholars argue that Jesus Christ's supernatural nature and His role as a normal man are mutually exclusive—that is, it is impossible for Jesus Christ to have Mary Magdalene as His loving wife, with kids, *and* be the Savior. What are they talking about? People, it is all the same thing. Each of us is supernatural, we are made of supernatural stuff, and, therefore, holograms ourselves. So please let Jesus Christ have a normal life! Regardless of how you may view the entity, Jesus Christ, His deep, supernatural message does not change. It is too beautiful and fundamental to change! Through extraordinarily deep meditation, Jesus Christ was in touch with Himself, His Father, and true identity at all times. No one has ever promoted peace as much and as correctly as He—this is an undeniable historical fact.

Scholarly comedy is also rampant in the evolution and creation discussion. People, it is all the same thing! The Universal Consciousness created local consciousness for its purposes, which often involves missions that exceed human comprehension. The local consciousness' mission is well-defined and requires local creativity. We are supposed to focus on this alone as long as we are creative. Therefore, evolution is a must as we were created for that purpose alone. So, please stop the nonsense of these futile secular arguments as we have far more important missions to fulfill than debate the stupidity of so many. Even "Scopes' Monkey" would laugh at the nonsense. The reason I write these words is because if they are ignored, other Ravensbrücks will happen again and again because we have not addressed the root causes of our problems.

As you may rightly say, none of this tells us why the "bad guys" exist. Why do accidents happen and take away our loved ones? It is all a matter of maintaining creativity at all cost. If there were no bad guys and no dramatic accidents, we humans would lose our creativity, our will, and ultimate reason for being who we are. In due time, the bad guy is destroyed as the Universal Consciousness unites the bad guy with his counterpart in the opposite universe. Once united, each will annihilate the other—like matter and antimatter. Of course, we haven't and can't observe that reaction and the true scenario may be very different from my weakly-human speculation. The bottom line is the Universal Consciousness has no memory of what was bad. It continues to move to far more important issues.

A measure of mankind's capability to successfully evolve is being able to minimize the bad guys and predict accidents. Given that benchmark, it becomes obvious that we have a long way to go as, my friends, we continually flounder in an ever-deepening swamp.

Yet, and this is worth emphasizing, we have the power of the Universal Consciousness in each of us. Albert Einstein felt it in his meditations. Again, we don't know how to read and assimilate it. God said once, "I created mankind in My own image." He could not have been clearer. So we visualize God as a human being, as shown in famous paintings, which is folly. Actually the reverse is true, we should visualize ourselves as the Universal Consciousness, which is our true identity. But this is easier said than done.

The conclusion is that we should look at ourselves in an entirely different way and be extraordinarily proud of who and what we are. And—I insist on this critically important point—*who we want to be*. No good person wakes up in the morning and consciously decides to become a bad person. Bad people become that way through the brutal arrogance of tyrants and rulers. They are misled by false and man-made holograms or suffer from malfunctioning brains.

"Good" people can be Christians, Muslims, Jews, Buddhists, animists, or atheists provided they, and we, respect each other's true self. We are all the same. Names and labels are only semantic. They are not the "real" person. If we elevate ourselves to where we belong, that is being our own selves, we can reach serenity and jointly collaborate on our individual and collective "true" missions. Then, and only then, can we prevent other Ravensbrücks from happening.

A young girl named Malala Yousafzai rightly said recently, "I have a right to speak, I have a right to play, and I have a right to an education." Obviously, her true identity is at work in a positive way. What a girl! Her Nobel Prize for peace was well-deserved and inspiring. We need many more people like her and we need to support and follow their lead.

Regardless of which side you are on, how is it that mankind can create a hell like Ravensbrück, September 11, 2001, or genocidal religious wars? The reason is clear, simple, and frightening. It is because we are slaves of a grand mistake made many thousands of years ago. Our forbearers enslaved themselves and their ability to independently think. We continue to remain in voluntary bondage when we follow tyrants and rulers who want to use us to mindlessly support their quests for power. Although many people kept their sanity (and goodness) throughout the millennia, many deviated by fanatically supporting false gods and leaders. As my good friend Charles Oliver Ingamells said so well, "There are among us those who perceive the flaws in the structure on which we build. We are advised to refrain from insulting and rejecting them. Listen to them! One or other of them may rescue us from the swamp in which we flounder."

When I was twenty-one, out of curiosity, I read Hitler's "Mein Kampf." Who in their right mind could write, much less believe and support those precepts? Who could have followed such sickness and folly? In Hitler's twisted writings, he tells the reader that the world must be ruled and exploited through intimidation and fear—exactly like today's terrorists. Of course, their leaders and congregants must commit to their self-defined master race/true religion. To advance in the organization, they will lie, betray, and assassinate as mandated by warped political or religious dogma. Through deceit, intimidation, propaganda, and misplaced allegiance, terror leaders forcefully gather the human fodder needed to further their evil causes.

How on earth, dear reader, could a country like Germany, which was (and is) full of extremely bright and critical people, fall for Hitler's guile, a psychologically and morally corrupt blathering? The explanation is simple. After Germany was defeated in 1918, it was economically ostracized and isolated to the point that only half its citizens had jobs. And, as history has taught, what is it that people do when they starve and no longer have anything to lose? They reach rage! Their empty stomachs overruled their brains and they came prepared to listen and follow this odd fellow who promises a revival and "return to the good old days." Forget the means to the end, it is only the end that counts. My friends, do you think anyone learned from Germany's lesson?

Believe it or not, we see this repeat again and again in Cuba, Korea, Russia, Iran, Syria. It never stops. And guess what? We will pay piper dearly! In other words, if you want to punish the tyrants, make sure your actions reform or obliterate their evil philosophies. But make certain you don't punish millions of innocent people in this process. This is precisely where we fail every time. Every time we fail, we create the breeding grounds for more new tyrants. Tyrants that often exceed the excesses of their predecessor. Witness: Assad, Hussein, and Khadafy.

Who we think we are is a millennia-old misperception. Who we really are is beautiful and simple. What we are and have is truly amazing. How is it conceivable we have so much yet do so little positive with it and damage so much of it?

My dear friends from around the world, let's get to work together. God, or the Universal Consciousness for those who don't believe in God, is waiting for us to wake up and live a normal, peaceful, and exciting life—full of love. And remember this statement, *a religion that does not promote peace as a core tenet, has nothing to offer.* So don't join those ranks! Furthermore, politicians who do not promote peace in their words and actions, have nothing to offer either. So don't vote for them!

I would like to finally add, *be aware of the slick negotiators who use words to obfuscate their true motives and goals*. They will invariably rationalize that doing nothing is best. They will lead us to anarchy; they should not be permitted to run our institutions or countries. Above all, beware of all forms of extremism, as they are formidable, destructive positions that taint and pervert all that they contact.

We urgently need to reinvent our ethics, our philosophies, and, above all, our politics. This is an awesome job but an absolute necessity.

What am I trying to say? What is the big picture? I believe each of us needs to change our respective life's paradigms. Why? Because each of us is a unique, single entity, a *"one."* As a one, we must cease being observers of life and change ourselves to become activists of one and to participate with others in their "oneness." As a community of "ones," our collective power can be absolutely astonishing and untapped. As an individual one, there is no need for so many borders other than those necessary for managing local jurisdictions, law enforcement, and cultures, which are and always will be essential. Further, there is no need for excessive race, religious beliefs, or political persuasions. There is no need for who you are, there is only a need for who you want to be: a peaceful, good, and inspiring person. Of course, and this is important, sometimes tough love is necessary and will always be necessary to guide us and protect our loved ones. I like that quote from Confucius (Kung Fu Tze),

"Good government is obtained when those who are near are made happy, and those who are far off are attracted."

I always found it fascinating that Aline's favorite piece of classical music was Concerto for Violin in D major by Ludwig van Beethoven, a German!

RECOMMENDED READINGS

Geneviève de Gaulle Anthoniz—La Traversée de la nuit. Editions du Seuil, 1998

Geneviève de Gaulle Anthoniz—the dawn of hope. Memoir of Ravensbrück. Editions du Seuil, 1998

Germaine Tillion—Ravensbrück, an eyewitness account of a women's concentration camp. Anchor Books, 1975

Jack. G. Morrison—Ravensbrück, Everyday life in a women's concentration camp 1939-1945. Markus Wiener Publishers, Princeton, 2000

Elie Wiesel—Winner of the Nobel Peace prize—Night. Hill and Wang, a division of Farrar, Straus and Giroux, New York, 2006

ABOUT THE AUTHOR

Dr. Francis F. Pitard, born in Normandy on February 5, 1942, is a consulting expert in sampling, statistical process control, and total quality management. He is president of Francis Pitard Sampling Consultants (www.fpscsampling.com) and Technical Director of Mineral Stats Inc. (www.mineralstats.com) in Broomfield, Colorado, USA. He provides consulting services in many countries. Dr. Pitard has six years of experience with the French Atomic Energy Commission and fifteen years with Amax Extractive R&D. He taught Sampling Theory for the Continuing Education Offices of Colorado School of Mines, the Australian Mineral Foundation, for the Mining Department of the University of Chile, and the University of Witwatersrand in South Africa. He has a doctorate in Technology from the Aalborg University in Denmark. He is author of several textbooks on Sampling Theory and Practice and two historical novels about Polynesians, Heirs of a Lost Race and Rapa Nui Settlers. These two novels explain how peace can be reached. He is the recipient of the prestigious Pierre Gy's Gold Medal for excellence in promoting and teaching the Theory of Sampling (Cape Town, South Africa, 2009). His hobby, among many others, is Nuclear Physics and the possibilities it offers to the future of our world.

CPSIA information can be obtained
at www.ICGtesting.com
Printed in the USA
FSOW03n0134070617
34797FS

9 781683 487289